DATE DUE

w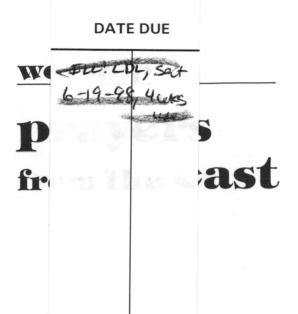

ILL: CDL, Sat
6-19-98, 4 wks

p

fr   the   ast

UPI 201-9509   PRINTED IN USA

worship

prayers
from the east

Bryan D. spinks

The Pastoral Press

Washington, DC

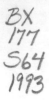
Acknowledgments

Acknowledgment is gratefully made to use again the following: "A Note on the Anaphora Outlined in Narsai's Homily XXXII," *Journal of Theological Studies*, New Series 31 (1980) 82-93; "The Original Form of the Anaphora of the Apostles: A Suggestion in the Light of Maronite Sharar," *Ephemerides Liturgicae* 91 (1977) 146-161; "Addai and Mari and the Institution Narrative: The Tantalizing Evidence of Gabriel Qatraya," *Ephemerides Liturgicae* 98 (1984) 60-67; "The East Syrian Anaphora of Theodore: Reflections upon Its Sources and Theology," *Ephemerides Liturgicae* 103 (1989) 441-455; "Eucharistic Offering in the East Syrian Anaphoras," *Orientalia Christiana Periodica* 50 (1984) 347-371; "Priesthood and Offering in the *Kuššāpê*, of the East Syrian Anaphoras," *Studia Liturgica* 15 (1983) 104-117.

ISBN: 1-56929-000-8

Contents

Introduction

As an undergraduate theology student at the University of Durham, I was first introduced to the East Syrian or "Nestorian" Eucharistic Prayer of Addai and Mari. Later, when I was pursuing post-graduate research in the English Calvinist liturgical tradition, I found time for "light relief" by learning Syriac under the tutelage of Sebastian Brock, and decided to look at Addai and Mari and what was then (1974) the recently published critical text of the Maronite version called *Sharar*. A small group of former liturgy students of Arthur Couratin formed the Durham Liturgical Group, and I read a paper at one of these small, informal meetings, which was later to appear in *Ephemerides Liturgicae*. And so began my continuing interest in the East Syrian liturgical tradition alongside a continuing interest in liturgy of the Reformed tradition. I am grateful to Lawrence Johnson and Virgil Funk of The Pastoral Press for responding so warmly to the suggestion that a number of my published papers be brought together in a single volume.

Chapter 1 is an expansion of the introduction to my English editions of the Anaphora of Addai and Mari as found in the *Mar Eša'ya* manuscript, which is our earliest manuscript of this liturgy, and of Maronite *Sharar*. This was originally published in 1980. It is mainly a review of the theories put forward by scholars regarding the reconstruction of the anaphora in a more "original form." Several studies have appeared since then, including the important study and text by Anthony Gelston. I have therefore taken the opportunity of bringing this survey up to date.

Chapter 2 is essentially the paper mentioned above, originally read to the Durham Liturgical Group in 1975, and subsequently published in *Ephemerides Liturgicae*. It represents my own venture into "textual reconstruction," though having changed my mind slightly on one point since 1975, I have taken the opportunity to rewrite that part of the original paper.

Chapter 3, published in the same journal in 1989, gives my reasons for rejecting the "certainty" of a missing institution narrative which some scholars have found for Addai and Mari.

Chapter 4 was intended to appear in tandem with my edited version of a paper on Theodore by the late Douglas Webb, but unfortunately they became separated, and Webb's paper appeared in the first issue of the next volume. My paper was published shortly before the critical text of Jacob Vadakkel appeared, and at the 1991 Oxford Patristic Congress Dr. Anthony Gelston read a Master Theme paper on the relationship of the Anaphora of Theodore with the Catechetical Lectures of Theodore of Mopsuestia. I have found nothing in the studies of Vadakkel and Gelston which required any changes in my article, and it has been republished without alteration.

Chapter 5 was written in response to some observations in a more general paper on eucharistic offering by my friend and colleague on the Church of England Liturgical Commission, Dr. Kenneth Stevenson. Chapter 7 was an extension of this study, and was originally read at the Vienna meeting of Societas Liturgica in 1983.

Chapter 8 was written with the conviction that Ratcliff's observations were wrong, though at the time I had no idea that I would one day offer lectures on liturgy in the very Divinity Faculty where as a Professor Ratcliff conceived his initial paper on Narsai's homilies.

Chapter 6 and 9 are fresh compositions and are published here for the first time. If some regard the East Syrian liturgical rites as rather too esoteric and academic, I hope that the final chapter illustrates their pertinence to the modern church, both in terms of ecclesiastical chauvinism and the problem of modernizing ancient texts.

Bryan D. Spinks

1

The Quest for the "Original Form" of the Anaphora of the Apostles Addai and Mari

FOR MANY YEARS NOW THE AREA OF EAST SYRIA HAS BEEN REGARDED AS important for liturgical research, both on account of its semitic background, and its later isolation from the rest of Christendom. A considerable number of recent studies have drawn attention to the Judaeo-Christian origin of Syriac-speaking Christianity which centered upon Edessa and Nisibis, and to the strong Jewish influence which was exerted from the region of Adiabene.[1] The *Peshitta*, the Syriac Old Testament, appears to have been a Jewish production, in fact another Targum; and the great Syrian theologians, Aphrahat and Ephraem, seem to have been considerably influenced by Jewish sectarian teaching.[2] Robert Murray suggests that, although the Syriac Church was definitely separated from Judaism by the fourth century, in certain important respects it still remained spiritually close to the parent synagogue.[3] Furthermore, this area had a long history of resisting repeated attempts to Hellenize it, and was strongly anti-Byzantine in spirit. After the Council of Ephesus in 431, many of the bishops of this area rejected the Christology of Cyril of Alexandria in favor of that of the deposed teacher, Nestorius, and as the Nestorian Church, it was later reorganized with its center at Nisibis in the Persian Empire, and was effectively insulated linguistically, culturally, and politically from the rest of Christendom.[4] Not unnaturally, therefore, liturgical scholars have paid particular attention to the liturgical tradition of the Edessene Church.

The East Syrian eucharistic tradition is represented by the anaphoras of the Apostles Addai and Mari, Theodore of Mopsuestia, and Nestorius. A fragment published by R.H. Connolly seems to belong to this tradition,[5] but others, if they actually existed, have since disappeared.[6] The anaphoras attributed to Theodore and Nestorius were certainly originally composed in Greek, and subsequently translated into Syriac. They show clear signs of West Syrian influence, and have received relatively little attention from liturgical scholars.[7]

However, quite the reverse is true of Addai and Mari, which is an original Syriac composition. Although the late Bayard H. Jones believed that it represents a précis of Nestorius, dating from the early seventh century,[8] most scholars, taking its semitic character more seriously, have dated it variously between the second and fourth centuries, and regard it as an important witness in understanding the growth and development of the early eucharistic prayer.[9]

THE EARLIEST TEXT OF ADDAI AND MARI

Addai and Mari is known in three textual traditions:

1. The Nestorian.

2. The Chaldean Church, having its center at Mosul, being that part of the Nestorian Church which became a Uniate Church in communion with Rome in the seventeenth century.

3. The Malabar Church in India, also a Uniate Church.

Prior to 1966 it seemed that only six manuscripts—two from about 1500, and four others of the sixteenth century—were available for establishing a critical text of this anaphora. That the list given by Brightman[10] was woefully inadequate was being established by the patient work of Douglas Webb of Wilburton, Ely, and by William F. Macomber in the United States.[11] In 1966 Macomber published a list of earlier manuscripts, together with a critical edition of Addai and Mari, based on the text from a *hudra* (the book containing the proper of the liturgy and of the offices for Sundays, feasts of Our Lord, and the principal saints' days) belonging to the Church of *Mar Eša'ya* in Mosul, which he dated as tenth/eleventh century.[12] So far this dating has not been challenged, and its text of Addai and Mari has been regarded as the earliest form of the anaphora that we presently have. The structure of the anaphoras as given in Brightman and in the *Mar Eša'ya* text can be summarized as follows:

[*Kuššāpâ* – a private prayer of the celebrant said kneeling and in a low voice.

Ghāntā – an inclination - a prayer said in a low voice and with inclined head.

Qanona – an audible conclusion to a Ghāntā.]

BRIGHTMAN (pp. 283-288)			MAR ESA'YA		
A.	Dialogue		A.	Dialogue	
	Kuššāpâ				
B.	Ghāntā	– Praise and Thanksgiving.	B.	Ghāntā	– Praise and Thanksgiving.
C.	Qanona	– *Sanctus* with its introduction.	C.	Qanona	– *Sanctus* with its introduction.
	Kuššāpâ				
D.	Ghāntā	– Thanksgiving for redemption.	D.	Ghāntā	– Thanksgiving for redemption.
	Qanona	– Doxology.		Qanona	– Doxology.
	Kuššāpâ				
E.	Ghāntā	– Commemoration of the righteous fathers. Petition for peace.	E.	Ghāntā	– Commemoration of the righteous fathers. Petition for peace.
F.		Petition for all the church.	F.		Petition for all the church.
G.		Commemoration of the mystery of Christ.	G.		Commemoration of the mystery of Christ.
H.		Epiclesis.	H.		Epiclesis.
I.	Qanona	– Doxology.	I.	Qanona	– Doxology.

Although there are some important verbal differences, the major difference is that the *Mar Eša'ya* text lacks the *Kuššāpê* intercessions.

The *Mar Eša'ya* Text

A.

And the priest says:	Peace be with you.
And they reply:	And with you and your spirit.
And the deacon says:	Give peace to one another in the love of Christ.
And they say:	For all the Catholikoi.
And the deacon proclaims:	Let us give thanks and intercede.

And the priest says:	The grace of Our Lord, etc.
And they reply:	Amen.
And the priest says:	Lift up your minds (May your minds be above).
And they reply:	Towards you, O God.
And the priest says:	The oblation is offered to God the Lord of all.
And they reply:	It is fit and right.
And the deacon says:	Peace be with us.

B.

And the priest recites quietly:
Worthy of praise from every mouth, and thanksgiving from every tongue is the adorable and glorious Name of the Father and the Son and of the Holy Spirit, who created the world by his grace and its inhabitants in his compassion, and redeemed mankind in his mercy, and has effected [lit. made] great grace towards mortals.

C.

Your majesty, O Lord, a thousand thousand heavenly beings worship and myriad myriads of angels, hosts of spiritual beings, ministers (of) fire and of spirit, with cherubim and holy seraphim, glorify your Name
Qanona. Crying out and glorifying
And they reply: Holy, Holy.

D.

And the priest recites quietly:
And with these heavenly powers we give thanks to you, O Lord, even we, your lowly, weak and miserable servants, because you have effected in us a great grace which cannot be repaid, in that you put on our humanity so as to quicken us by your divinity. And you lifted up our poor estate, and righted our fall. And you raised up our mortality. And you forgave our debts. You justified our sinfulness and you enlightened our understanding. And you, our Lord and our God, vanquished our enemies and made triumphant the lowliness of our weak nature through the abounding compassion of your grace.
Qanona. And for all
And they reply: Amen.
And the deacon says: In your minds.

E.

And the priest recites quietly:
You, O Lord, in your unspeakable mercies make a gracious remembrance for all the upright and just fathers who have been pleasing before you in the commemoration of the body and blood of your Christ which we offer to you upon the pure and holy altar as you have taught us. And grant us your tranquility and your peace all the days of the world. *Repeat.*
And they reply: Amen.

F.

That all the inhabitants of the earth may know that you alone are God, the true Father, and you have sent our Lord Jesus Christ, your Son and your beloved, and he, our Lord and our God, taught us in his life-giving gospel all the purity and holiness of the prophets, apostles, martyrs and confessors and bishops and priests and deacons, and of all the children of the holy catholic church, who have been marked with the mark of holy baptism.

G.

And we also, O Lord,—*Thrice*—your lowly, weak and miserable servants who are gathered together and stand before you at this time have received by tradition of the example which is from you rejoicing, and glorifying, and magnifying, and commemorating and praising, and performing this great and dread mystery of the passion and death and resurrection of our Lord Jesus Christ.

H.

May he come, O Lord, your Holy Spirit and rest upon this oblation (*of*)
And the deacon says: Be in silence:
of your servants, and bless and hallow it, that it may be to us, O Lord, for the pardon of debts and the forgiveness of sins, and a great hope of resurrection from the dead and a new life in the kingdom of heaven with all who have been pleasing before you.

I.

And for all your marvelous economy towards us we give you thanks and praise you without ceasing in your Church redeemed by the precious blood of your Christ, with open mouths and with uncovered faces.

Qanona. As we offer up
And they reply: Amen.
And they conclude everything as it is written in the Anaphora of the Interpreter, which (?) is written (?) (holy?) Sunday of the Annunciation.

SOME TEXTUAL PROBLEMS OF ADDAI AND MARI

By far the most puzzling textual problem of Addai and Mari is the apparent absence of any institution narrative. The East Syrian manuscripts, including *Mar Eša'ya*, lack an institution narrative. In the Urmiah Missal of Archbishop of Canterbury's mission, 1890, printed for the Nestorians, the editors inserted 1 Corinthians 11:23-25 at a point which seemed suitable, namely, before the *Kuššāpâ* "O Lord of Hosts, accept this offering," and the *ghāntā* commemorating the righteous fathers (E). Similarly, in the Catholic Chaldean Missal (Mosul, 1901 and 1936) an institution narrative has been inserted in the middle of the post-*Sanctus* prayer (D). In neither instance is there any manuscript authority for such insertions.

This apparent omission in the manuscripts finds confirmation in the Malabar liturgy. By means of a detailed concordance R.H. Connolly and Edmund Bishop illustrated that the Malabar liturgy was essentially the same liturgy as Addai and Mari; they were in fact one and the same liturgy.[13] The present Malabar use which goes back to the printed missal of 1774 (Rozian), and the version of the rite published by Antonio de Gouvea in 1606 (Menezian),[14] both contain an institution narrative, but after the anaphora and before the fraction (the two versions differ over the precise location). An earlier Malabrese manuscript, *Vat. Syr. 66*, attributed to Mar Joseph Sulaqa, Metropolitan of India 1556-1569, contains a narrative before the liturgy which the author intended to be recited at the end of the ceremonies of the fraction. Thus the rite of Malabar witnesses to the fact that on its arrival in India, the Anaphora of Addai and Mari contained no institution narrative. Did it ever contain such a narrative, and if it did, when and why was it removed?

Another problem is raised by the fact that part of Addai and Mari is addressed to the Father, and part to the Son. Was the author a muddle-headed monarchian, or does it represent later re-writing? Paragraph G, which commemorated the mystery of Christ, has no main verb, and it is not clear as to the identity and function of this prayer. A number of studies have questioned the antiquity of the intercessions, the *Sanctus*, and the epiclesis (C, E, F, H). These problems have resulted in repeated attempts to reconstruct a "primitive" text of Addai and Mari.

TEXTUAL RECONSTRUCTION BEFORE
THE *Mar Eša'ya* TEXT

E.C. Ratcliff

In the very influential article published in 1929, E.C. Ratcliff attempted to reconstruct the eucharistic prayer of the old Edessene Church which he believed was embedded in Addai and Mari.[15] Accepting that Addai and Mari had never contained an institution narrative, he questioned much of the remainder of the prayer in the manuscript tradition represented by the version of Brightman. Arguing from the outline given in Narsai's liturgical homilies, and following up a suggestion of Edmund Bishop, Ratcliff excised both the *Kuššāpâ* and *ghāntā* intercessions.[16] Of the remaining text, he believed the *Sanctus* and the epiclesis to be later interpolations, in both cases because the clauses introducing them appeared to have no connection with what preceded them, though he allowed that the epiclesis may have once occupied a position outside the anaphora.[17] The doxology after the second *ghāntā* which divided the anaphora in two he suggested was a doublet introduced on account of the intruding intercessions. Furthermore, in paragraph G, he suggested that the words "great and fearful and holy and lifegiving and divine" should be omitted as destroying the balance of the antithesis between "example" and "likeness" (Brightman = mystery). With the removal of the redundant post-*Sanctus* phrase "with these heavenly hosts," Ratcliff recast the pattern of Addai and Mari as a single prayer of three paragraphs: an address of praise to the name of the creator and redeemer; a thanksgiving for what he has done for humankind; a solemn following of Christ's example and a special commemoration of his redemptive death and resurrection, for which again praise and thanksgiving are offered to the divine name. He suggested that the prayer, originally addressed to Christ, was essentially a hymn of thanksgiving, and labelled it a "*eucharistia*," a rite which came somewhere in between the Mass and the agape.

Gregory Dix

Gregory Dix accepted much of Ratcliff's suggested reconstruction: the prayer was originally addressed to Christ; the preface and *Sanctus*, the intercessions and first doxology were interpolations. However, on two important points Dix differed from Ratcliff. In paragraph G, where the grammar is difficult because there is no main verb, and the address changes from the Son to the Father, he suggested the words "rejoicing, glorifying . . . Christ" were a later interpolation. Dix also defended the authenticity of the epiclesis, arguing that the Holy Spirit here was to be equated with the *shekinah* rather than the third person of the Trinity.[18]

Bernard Botte

In an article published in 1949, and later modified and elaborated in 1965,[19] Bernard Botte analyzed Addai and Mari. He argued that its style, characterized by a constant parallelism, betrays its semitic origin and its early date. He accepted Ratcliff's arguments concerning the *Sanctus* and the introductory words of paragraph D, and likewise his views on the intercessions and epiclesis—though the latter showed clear signs of being a semitic composition, and not a copy from Greek sources. He did not accept that the anaphora was originally addressed to the Son, but rather that the oscillation between Father and Son reflects unconscious monarchianism. However, Botte found it strange that an anaphora should contain neither an institution narrative nor an epiclesis. He noted the difficulty in translating paragraph G where, with one exception, the verbs are participles with the prenominal suffix. Brightman had translated it thus:

> And we also, O my Lord, thy weak and frail and miserable servants who are gathered together in thy name, both stand before thee at this time and have received the example which is from thee delivered unto us, rejoicing and praising and exalting and commemorating and celebrating this great and fearful and holy and lifegiving and divine mystery of the passion and the death and the burial and the resurrection of our Lord and our Saviour Jesus Christ.

Botte, however, gave it a slightly different rendering:

> And we also, O Lord, thy weak and frail and miserable servants who are gathered together in thy name and stand before thee at this time, we also have received by tradition the Type (Latin; French = *l'example*) which is from thee, rejoicing . . .[20]

Botte found a hiatus at the beginning of this paragraph, and the words seemed to him to require a foregoing sentence. Furthermore, the last part of the paragraph, "commemorating . . . resurrection" recalls the phraseology found in the classical anamnesis which follows an institution narrative. In Theodore an anamnesis is found which has similar wording to the paragraph of Addai and Mari, but there it follows an institution narrative which has a peculiar form:

> And with his holy Apostles in that night in which he was betrayed, he celebrated this great and holy and divine mystery, taking the bread in his holy hands. And he blessed and broke, and gave it to his disciples, and said, This is my body which is broken for the life of the world for the remission of sins. After the same manner also he gave thanks over the cup, and gave it to them, and said, This is my blood of the New Testament which is shed for many for the remission of sins. Take all of you therefore. Eat of this bread and drink of this cup. Do this whensoever you come together for my memorial.

> And as we have been commanded, so we your lowly, weak and miserable servants have come together, that by permission of your grace we may celebrate this great and awful and holy and divine mystery, wherein great salvation was wrought for the whole human race. (From the Urmiah edition.)

Botte also noted references to the institution narrative in Ephraem and Aphrahat where the ending was "whenever you are gathered together in my name." Paragraph G of Addai and Mari would seem to follow on from a particular Syriac form of narrative, and Botte identified it as an anamnesis. The conclusion he drew from this is that the anamnesis is the record of an institution narrative that has since disappeared. He suggested three phases of development:

1. Thanksgiving and recital of institution with anamnesis.
2. Thanksgiving and shortened recital of institution and epiclesis.
3. Thanksgiving and epiclesis without recital of institution.

In his article of 1965 Botte suggested a reordering of the text of Addai and Mari to bring it in line with those of Theodore and Nestorius—thanksgiving, institution, anamnesis, intercessions, epiclesis.

Most of Botte's recommendations have been endorsed by Louis Bouyer, who provides a reconstructed text with institution narrative according to the former's suggestions of 1965.[21]

H. Engberding

Whereas most scholars have regarded the intercessions of Addai and Mari as later interpolations, more caution was shown by H. Engberding,[22] who compared them with the intercessions of the other two East Syrian anaphoras, and an anaphora of the Maronite Church (the Syrian Church which is mainly located in Lebanon, and which since the time of the crusades has been a Uniate Church), called The Anaphora of St. Peter III, or *Sharar*.[23]

He concluded that the intercessions constitute part of the earliest form of the prayer, and that a doublet of petitions resulted from a borrowing of the intercessions of Theodore. Furthermore, Engberding disputed the identification of paragraph G as an anamnesis. He found similar constructions spread widely in the intercessions where, after a prayer for the dead, there occurs one for the living introduced by "We also." A very similar paragraph is found in Nestorius. According to Engberding, paragraph G is a continuation of the prayer for the living and forms part of the intercessions. It is not an anamnesis, and therefore there is no place which invites an institution narrative; Addai and Mari's original structure was praise and petition.

Bayard H. Jones

In a paper which was published posthumously, Bayard H. Jones[24] examined the history of the references to Addai and Mari in Syrian literature, and the history of its title, and argued that it was a précis of Nestorius resulting from the reforms which are alleged to have been made by Iso'yabh III (649-659) in the seventh century. The "primitive" form of Addai and Mari is *Nestorius*.

THE *MAR ESA'YA* TEXT OF ADDAI AND MARI

Concluding his article of 1965, Botte wrote, "short of a sensational discovery, we will always be in doubt."[25] The following year W.F. Macomber published what has come to be regarded as "a sensational discovery," namely, the text of Addai and Mari in a *hudra* of the Church of *Mar Eša'ya*, which on paleographical grounds he dated to the tenth or eleventh century—five centuries earlier than the text used by Ratcliff and Botte.[26] The broad characteristics of this text are as follows:

1. The anaphora lacks the *Kuššāpâ* intercessions. Although one of the features of the *hudra* is abbreviation, and although another early manuscript discovered by Macomber, the twelfth-century Diarbekir *hudra*, does not contain them, Macomber concluded that these intercessions were not generally introduced into the East Syrian liturgy before the end of the thirteenth century, and that Ratcliff's suggestions on this matter were correct.

2. The *Sanctus* is contained in the *Mar Eša'ya* text, but Macomber accepted Ratcliff's opinion that it was a later addition to the anaphora.

3. There is no institution narrative—Macomber suggested that it was removed by a reform carried out by Iso'yab III.

4. The phrase "in your name" upon which Botte built much of his argument for an institution narrative, is absent; also the word "and" introducing the epiclesis is absent, a point which Ratcliff regarded as supporting his view that this section was not original to the anaphora.[27]

No one has challenged Macomber's dating of the *Mar Eša'ya* text, and liturgical scholars seem to have accepted without question that its readings are to be preferred to those of other manuscripts.

MARONITE *SHARAR*

The close relationship that exists between Addai and Mari and the Maronite anaphora called *Sharar* was pointed out long ago by I.E. Rahmani and A. Baumstark, and had been investigated by Engberding.[28] Most of Addai and Mari is contained in *Sharar*, and the relationship points to a common origin, or a common source underlying both anaphoras.

In publishing the *Mar Eša'ya* text, Macomber provided the first critical text of Addai and Mari, and included readings of *Sharar* among the variant readings. In a later article Macomber made a comparison between Addai and Mari and *Sharar* with regard to three points.[29]

1. The prefatory dialogue. According to Macomber, Addai and Mari has been influenced by and expanded from Theodore. The East Syrian blessing of the oil of baptism seems to preserve an earlier form. By comparing it with the dialogue of *Sharar*, Macomber offered a reconstruction of the common source used by the two anaphoras.

2. Since the whole of *Sharar* from the post-*Sanctus* to the final doxology is addressed to the Son, Macomber accepted Ratcliff's opinion that Addai and Mari too was originally addressed to the Son. The pre-*Sanctus* has been adapted to praise the Trinity.

3. The Maronite anaphora contains an institution account, having a peculiar form, addressed to the Son, and embedded in intercessions in a block coming between paragraphs corresponding to E and F of Addai and Mari. Macomber suggested that the Maronite anaphora has preserved both the location and form of the institution narrative now absent from Addai and Mari.

The common source, he has argued further, was an anaphora of the Aramaic-speaking Church which had its center at Edessa. After the schism of the fifth century, it was preserved in the East Syrian Church, and the Aramaic-speaking areas of Lebanon and the Orontes valley.[30]

TEXTUAL RECONSTRUCTION OF THE ANAPHORA OF THE APOSTLES

For his comparison of the two anaphoras, Macomber had to use the text of *Sharar* in a Maronite missal of 1594, as no critical edition existed. This gap was filled in 1973 when J.M. Sauget published a critical text in the series *Anaphorae Syriacae*.[31] With good texts of both anaphoras being available, recent studies have been concerned with reconstructing the common source, the anaphora of the apostles, rather than simply proposing emendations to Addai and Mari.

In their general studies of the origin of the eucharistic prayer, Louis Ligier, Louis Bouyer, and Thomas Talley[32] have regarded the three *Ghānatā* of Addai and Mari as corresponding to the three *berakoth* of *Didache 10*, and behind them both, the three *berakoth* of the Jewish meal prayer, the *birkat ha-mazon*. Accepting this correspondence, and building on the suggestions of Macomber, reconstructions have been offered by José Manuel Sánchez Caro[33] and H.A.J. Wegman.[34]

Sánchez Caro reconstructs the text as follows:

> Paragraph B,   without any reference to Father, Son, and
> Spirit.
> D.
> E,   excluding "who have been pleasing in your sight,"
> "your Messiah" and the petition for peace.
> adding "as you have taught us *through your
> holy gospel.*"
> Institution narrative, from *Sharar*.
> Anamnesis, based on *Sharar* and G.
> F,   reconstructed.
> I.

The reconstructed prayer begins by addressing God in the second person, and then switches to the third person, which is explained as following the pattern of Jewish *berakoth*. Sánchez Caro suggests that later evolution of the text saw the introduction of the *Sanctus*, borrowed from the *Qedussah de Yoser* of the synagogue morning service, and an epiclesis; later still, reference to the Trinity was introduced into B. After the fifth-century schisms, the anaphora developed differently in the two Churches, and the East Syrian version lost its institution narrative, probably in the liturgical reform of Iso'yabh III.

Herman Wegman has also offered a reconstruction of the "primitive" form of the prayer. In his opinion the prayer was a table prayer in four strophes, comparable to the *Didache 10* and the *Birkat ha-mazon*, the fourth strophe being a kind of *chatimah* or concluding doxology. The prayer consisted of paragraphs

B, without reference to the Trinity.
D.
E.
I.

A second stage of development saw the introduction of an institution narrative (preserved in *Sharar*), with anamnesis and epiclesis (G and H). In his opinion F represents an even later addition.

A. Verheul similarly offered a reconstruction based on the *birkat ha-mazon*. He argued that its original form was of four sections:

B.
D. + G.
H.
I.

These correspond to the three *berakoth* of the Jewish meal prayer and its final *chatimah*. Verheul is dependent upon Wegman whom he cites.[35]

While many scholars have seen a tripartite structure in Addai and Mari, Jacob Vellian has drawn attention to the similarities in structure and theme which exist between Addai and Mari and the synagogue morning *berakoth* before the *Shema*, the *Yoser*, and the *Ahabah*. *Yoser* gives praise for creation and ends with the *Qedussah* (Isaiah 6:3); the *Ahabah* is a recalling of the gifts of God's love, such as the Torah and the land; it includes a commemoration of the fathers, and has a petition for peace. The doxologies of Addai and Mari divide the anaphora in two: the first part, A.-D., has a similar focus to *Yoser* with *Qedussah*, adding a general commemoration of the economy of Christ. There are also similarities between the themes of E., F., and I., and of the *Ahabah*. Vellian writes:

> If we follow the pattern of the morning *berakoth* in question, we may not find any place which explicitly invites the Institution-Narrative. So it could be that the Anaphora of Addai and Mari, which does not give any glimpse of the Institution-Narrative prior to the sixteenth century, was composed after the pattern of the morning *berakoth*.[36]

In 1982 W.F. Macomber published his reconstruction of the "original form" of the anaphora underlying Addai and Mari and the Maronite *Sharar*.[37] He argued that it dates at least from the third or fourth century, and possibly even the second century. He also expressed the view that often the Maronite version has retained the more archaic readings. He believed that the anaphora was originally addressed to the Son, and that the narrative of institution in *Sharar* may represent the substance of what was found in the common version. In his reconstruction he has accepted that some of the material which occurs only in the Maronite anaphora as being original, and likewise one section which occurs only in the East Syrian anaphora. He includes the epiclesis in brackets, suggesting that it was a fourth-century addition. He thus gives the following:

A. (emended in the light of the Maronite version).
B.
C.
D.
E.   (Maronite version which includes:
 – institution narrative;
 – anamnesis;
 – intercessions).
F.   (Maronite version).
G.
(H.)
I.

Jean Magne[38] in 1987 published a study of the two versions of the anaphora, and proposed a reconstruction as follows:

A.
B.
C.
E.
D.
H. + the last versicle of A. as an introduction.

Underlying this there are, according to Magne, two independent hymns (B. and C.). The stages of the additions were:

1. The addition of D to C;
2. The addition of intercessions and the oblation/epiclesis to B.
3. An interpolation of the commemoration and offering of the passion.
4. The fusion of the *Sanctus* and the post-*Sanctus* with the rest of the developing anaphora.

In 1989 William Marston published a very short study arguing (with very little evidence) that the anaphora had originally been based upon the Lord's Prayer, and was perhaps a thanksgiving for that prayer. His reconstruction[39] utilized:

A.
C.
D.
E.
F./G.   reformulated.
I.

The most recent study to date is that of Anthony Gelston of the University of Durham; Gelston provides an eclectic text of the East Syrian anaphora, based upon the medieval manuscripts.[40] He is not convinced of the *birkat ha-mazon* links, the synagogal parallels, the reconstructions of Magne, or the Marston proposal. He is also suspicious of attaching too much weight to the Maronite text, and rejects Macomber's estimation of the institution narrative of *Sharar*. The study includes an introduction and commentary, and a very cautious proposed reconstruction. He accepts that the Maronite opening dialogue is more original, but argues that the anaphora was originally addressed to the Father. Where the anaphora seems to address the Son, this he argues should be interpreted in the light of 2 Corinthians 5:19. However, Gelston does suggest reordering the intercessions E.-F. with the help of the fragment published by Connolly. He reconstructs the text thus:

> Do thou, O my Lord, in thy manifold mercies
> make a good remembrance for all the upright and just fathers,
> the prophets and apostles and martyrs and confessors,
> in the commemoration of the body and blood of thy Christ,
> which we offer to thee upon the pure and holy altar,
> as thou hast taught us in his life-giving Gospel.
> And make with us thy tranquility and thy peace all the
>   days of the age,
> that all the inhabitants of the world may know thee,
> that thou alone art God the true Father,
> and thou didst send our Lord Jesus Christ thy Son and
>   thy Beloved.
> And may they stand before thee in all purity and holiness,
> the bishops and priests and deacons
> and all the children of the holy Church
> signed with the sign of holy baptism.

AN ORIGINAL FORM?

The publication of the *Mar Eša'ya* text of Addai and Mari and of a critical text of *Sharar* has encouraged renewed speculation on the anaphora of the apostles, and the quest for its "original text." At present there is no consensus regarding solutions to all the problems which the texts present. As Emmanuel Cutrone puts it, "it is only painfully obvious that there is still mystery and enigma associated with Addai and Mari."[41] However, it is possible that attempts to reconstruct a single "original text" are misleading, and that we can do no more than identify the common material found in the two anaphoras. Writing on the Jewish *berakoth*, Joseph Heinemann emphasized:

> We must not try to determine by philological methods the "original" text of any prayer without first determining whether or not such an "original" text ever existed. For we are dealing with materials which originated as part of an oral tradition and hence by their very nature were not phrased in any fixed uniform formulation—which at a later stage came to be "revised" and expanded—but rather were improvised on the spot; and, subsequently, "re-improvised" and reworded in many different formulations in an equally spontaneous fashion.[42]

Early eucharistic prayers may have followed some outline, but they were the free composition of the bishop or president.[43] If the Anaphora of the Apostles is early, and if we are to take its semitic background seriously, it may be that we have two developed, or "re-improvised" and reworded versions of a once oral tradition. It is perhaps more accurate to speak of a common tradition rather than of an "original text."

Notes

1. For the literature, see Robert Murray, *Symbols of Church and Kingdom: A Study in Early Syriac Tradition* (Cambridge: Cambridge University Press, 1975).

2. Ibid.

3. Ibid.

4. See Gregory Dix, *The Shape of the Liturgy* (London: Dacre Press, Adam and Charles Black, 1945) 173-178.

5. R.H. Connolly, "Sixth-Century Fragments of an East Syrian Anaphora," *Oriens Christianus*, New Series 12-14 (1925) 99-128.

6. F.E. Brightman and C.E. Hammond, *Liturgies Eastern and Western*, vol. 1. *Eastern Liturgies* (Oxford: Oxford University Press, 1896) lxxx.

7. F.E. Brightman, "The Anaphora of Theodore," *Journal of Theological Studies* 31 (1930) 160-164; Bayard H. Jones, "The Sources of the Nestorian Liturgy," *Anglican Theological Review* 46 (1964) 414-425; Bayard H. Jones, "The Formation of the Nestorian Liturgy," *Anglican Theological Review* 48 (1966) 276-306; L. Bouyer, *Eucharist*, tr. C.U. Quinn (Notre Dame: Notre Dame University Press, 1968) 342ff; B. Botte, "Les anaphores syriennes orientales," in *Eucharisties d'orient et d'occident*, vol. 2 (Paris: Les Editions du Cerf, 1970). For more recent studies, see chapter 4.

8. Bayard H. Jones, "The History of the Nestorian Liturgies," *Anglican Theological Review* 46 (1964) 157-176, esp. 174.

9. B. Botte, "L'anaphore chaldéenne des apôtres," *Orientalia Christiana Periodica* 15 (1949) 259-276; W.F. Macomber, "The Ancient Form of the Anaphora of the Apostles," in *East of Byzantium: Syria and Armenia in the Formative Period*, ed. N.G. Garsoian, T.F. Mathews, and R.W. Thompson (Washington, D.C.: Dumbarton Oaks Center for Byzantine Studies, 1982) 73-88.

10. Brightman, *Liturgies Eastern and Western* lxxix.

11. For their respective results, D. Webb, "Variations dans les versions manuscrites de la liturgie nestorienne d'Addai et Mari," *Sacris Eruditi* 18 (1967-1968) 478-523; W.F. Macomber, "The Oldest Known Text of the Anaphora of the Apostles Addai and Mari," *Orientalia Christiana Periodica* 32 (1966) 335-371.

12. Macomber, "The Oldest Known Text."

13. R.H. Connolly, E. Bishop, "The Work of Menezes on the Malabar Liturgy," *Journal of Theological Studies* 15 (1914) 396-425, 569-589; F.C. Burkitt, "The Old Malabar Liturgy," *Journal of Theological Studies* 29 (1928) 155-157.

14. Placid of St. Joseph, "The Present Syro-Malabar Liturgy: Menezian or Rozian?" *Orientalia Christiana Periodica* 23 (1957) 313-331.

15. E.C. Ratcliff, "The Original Form of the Anaphora of Addai and Mari: A Suggestion," *Journal of Theological Studies* 30 (1928-1929) 23-32.

16. Ibid.

17. In fact, at a later date Ratcliff's private opinion was that the original form of Addai and Mari had concluded with the *Sanctus*. See my essay "The Cleansed Leper's Thankoffering before the Lord: Edward Craddock Ratcliff and the Pattern of the Early Anaphora," in *The Sacrifice of Praise*, ed. Bryan D. Spinks (Rome: CLV- Edizioni Liturgiche, 1981) 161-178.

18. Dix, *The Shape of the Liturgy* 184.

19. B. Botte, "L'anaphore chaldéene des apôtres"; B. Botte, "Problèmes de l'anaphore syrienne des apôtres Addaï et Mari," *L'Orient syrien* 10 (1965) 89-106.

20. The English translation here tries to do justice to Botte's Latin (1949) and French (1965) translations, and his discussion of terminology (1949), pp. 267-268.

21. Bouyer, *Eucharist* 147-158.

22. H. Engberding, "Zum anaphorischen Fürbittgebet der Ostsyrischen Liturgie der Apostel Addaj und Mar(j)," *Oriens Christianus* 41 (1957) 102-124.

23. *Sharar*, meaning "confirm" or "strengthen," is a title given to this anaphora, it being the opening word of a prayer of the pre-anaphora.

24. See note 8 above.

25. Botte, "Problèmes" 106.

26. The precise setting is difficult since there is no reproduction available of a dated sample of the so-called "Nestorian" cursive writing earlier than 1243 A.D. While some parts of the manuscript are thirteenth-century additions, the original part is older, and a marginal note is written in a hand which resembles two lines of British Library *Add. Ms. 17,923*, dated 1074 A.D.

27. See my essay cited in note 17 above.

28. I.E. Rahmani, *Testamentum Domini Nostri Jesu Christi* (Mosul, 1899); A. Baumstark, "Altlibanesische Liturgie," *Oriens Christianus* 29 (1932) 32-48; H. Engberding, "Urgestalt, Eingenart und Entwicklung eines altantiochenischen eucharistischen Hochgebetes," *Oriens Christianus* 29 (1932) 32-48.

29. W.F. Macomber, "The Maronite and Chaldean Versions of the Anaphora of the Apostles," *Orientalia Christiana Periodica* 37 (1971) 55-84.

30. W.F. Macomber, "A Theory on the Origins of the Syrian, Maronite and Chaldean Rites," *Orientalia Christiana Periodica* 39 (1973) 235-242.

31. *Anaphorae Syriacae*, vol. 2, fasc. 3 (Rome: Pontificium Institutum Orientalium Studiorum, 1973) 275-323.

32. L. Ligier, "The Origins of the Eucharistic Prayer: From the Last Supper to the Eucharist," *Studia Liturgica* 9 (1973) 161-185; L. Bouyer, *Eucharist* 154-155; T.J. Talley, "The Eucharistic Prayer of the Ancient Church according to Recent Research: Results and Reflections," *Studia Liturgica* 11 (1976) 138-158.

33. J.M. Sánchez Caro, "La anáfora de Addai y Mari y la anfora meronita šarrar: intento de reconstrucción de la fuente primitiva común," *Orientalia Christiana Periodica* 43 (1977) 41-69.

34. H.A.J. Wegman, "Pleidooi voor een Teskst de Anaphora van de Apostelen Addai en Mari," *Bijdragen* 40 (1979) 15-43.

35. A. Verheul, "La prière eucharistique de Addaï et de Mari," *Questions Liturgiques* 61 (1980) 19-27.

36 J. Vellian, "The Anaphora Structure of Addai and Mari Compared to the Berakoth Preceding the Shema in the Synagogue Morning Service Contained in the Seder R. Amram Gaon," *Le Muséon* 85 (1972) 201-223.

37. W.F. Macomber, "The Ancient Form of the Anaphora of the Apostles."

38. J. Magne, "L'Anaphore nestorienne dite d'Addée et Mari et l'anaphore maronite dite de Pierre III: Etude comparative," *Orientalia Christiana Periodica* 53 (1987) 107-158.

39. W. Marston, "A Solution to the Enigma of Addai and Mari," *Ephemerides Liturgicae* 103 (1989) 79-91.

40. A. Gelston, *The Eucharistic Prayer of Addai and Mari* (Oxford: Clarendon Press, 1992).

41. E. Cutrone, "The Anaphora of the Apostles: Implications of the Mar Esay'ya Text," *Theological Studies* 43 (1973) 624-642, 642.

42. J. Heinemann, *Prayer in the Talmud: Forms and Patterns* (New York and Berlin: Walter De Gruyter, 1977) 42.

43. R.P.C. Hanson, "The Liberty of the Bishop to Improvise Prayer in the Eucharist," *Vigiliae Christianae* 15 (1961) 173-175; A. Bouley, *From Freedom to Formula* (Washington, D.C.: Catholic University of America Press, 1981).

2

The Original Form of the Anaphora of the Apostles: A Suggestion in the Light of Maronite *Sharar*

AMONG MODERN LITURGICAL SCHOLARS THE LATE DR. BAYNARD H. JONES seems to stand conspicuously alone in his belief that Addai and Mari is merely a précis of the Anaphora of Nestorius, dating from the early seventh century.[1] Most scholars, taking its semitic character more seriously, have recognized this East Syrian Liturgy as an important witness to the early pattern of the anaphora.[2] Whereas for Dr. Jones the absence of an institution narrative might easily be explained as a mark of the extravagance of the abbreviator, and is of little consequence, for those who accept an early dating it still poses a problem concerning the shape and content of the early eucharistic prayer.

The textual problem is well known, but for convenience we may briefly restate it.

The East Syrian manuscripts of Addai and Mari lack an institution narrative, and in the Urmiah Missal for the Archbishop of Canterbury's Mission, 1890, the editors inserted 1 Corinthians 11:23-25 at a point which seemed suitable, namely, before the *Kuššāpâ* "O Lord of Hosts, accept this offering," and the *ghāntā* commemorating the "just and righteous fathers." Similarly in the Catholic Chaldean Missal (Mosul, 1901 and 1936) a narrative has been inserted in the middle of the post-*Sanctus* prayer before the Christological prayer "we your weak, frail and miserable servants." In neither instance is there any manuscript authority for such insertions.

This apparent omission in the manuscript tradition finds confirmation in the Syro-Malabar liturgy. By means of a detailed concordance R.H. Connolly and Edmund Bishop illustrated that the Malabar liturgy was essentially the same as the liturgy of Addai and Mari; they were in fact one and the same liturgy.[3] In this case, however, an institution narrative was to be found, but after the anaphora and before the faction.[4] This strange positioning confirmed that at least since the fifteenth century no institution narrative was contained within the anaphora.

The discovery of the *Mar Eša'ya* manuscript at Mosul, now the earliest known manuscript of Addai and Mari, confirms that this is true also of the tenth or eleventh century.[5]

Has an institution narrative dropped out of the anaphora, and if so, what was its position and why did it drop out? Or did the anaphora quite simply never contain an institution narrative?

In his influential article on the original structure of Addai and Mari, Professor E.C. Ratcliff, accepting that it had never contained an institution narrative, questioned much of the remainder of the anaphora in the manuscript tradition represented by the version of Brightman in *Liturgies Eastern and Western*.[6] On the authority of Edmund Bishop, Ratcliff excised not only the *Kuššāpâ* intercessions, but also those of the *ghāntā*.[7] Of the remainder of the text, he believed the *Sanctus* and the epiclesis to be later additions, and the doxology after the *post*-Sanctus which divides the anaphora into two, he suggested was a doublet introduced on account of the intruding intercessions.[8] Observing that Addai and Mari was in part addressed to the Trinity and in part to the Son, Ratcliff wished to reduce the anaphora to three paragraphs addressed to Christ, and labelled it a "*eucharistia*," a rite which came somewhere in between the Mass and the agape.[9]

When Ratcliff's suggestions are compared with the *Mar Eša'ya* text, they find support only in the removal of the *Kuššāpâ* intercessions. The *ghāntā* for the righteous fathers and the church, the *Sanctus*, the epiclesis and the two doxologies are all contained in the oldest manuscript, and it gives no support for their removal.

An objection to this comparison might be that Ratcliff was concerned with the original structure of the prayer in the second or third century, and not as it had developed in the tenth or eleventh century. But the antiquity of the *Mar Eša'ya* text and the date of the manuscripts containing it are not necessarily the same. The possibility of a second century A.D. dating for the *Mar Eša'ya* text has been partly established by the work of Fr. Jacob Vellian in which he has drawn attention to the close affinities which exist both in structure and themes between it and the two *berakoth* preceding the *shema* of the synagogue morning service, the *Yoser* and *Ahabah*.[10]

Yoser, which is the first part of the morning *berakoth*, is centered on the commemoration of creation and on the *Qedussah*. The first part of Addai and Mari has the same points of focus, to which is added a general commemoration of the economy of Christ. Of particular note is the striking similarity in expression between the *Qedussah* and *Sanctus*.

The *Ahabah*, the second part of the morning *berakoth*, is an anamnesis of the gifts of God's love such as the Torah and the land; it contains a commemoration of the fathers, refers to the teaching of the statutes, and has a petition for peace. The similarities are quite remarkable.

Strangely enough, Vellian does not discuss the dating of the two Jewish *berakoth*, a factor which would seem essential for his thesis, since the text he uses is that of the eighth-century A.D. *Seder Amram Gaon*. The validity of the comparison rests on the two synagogue *berakoth* either antedating or being contemporaneous with Addai and Mari. In fact, Vellian's comparison cannot be entirely accepted. The forms of the *Yoser* and *Ahabah* which he gives from the *Seder Amram Gaon*, and which are almost identical to those in Singer's *Daily Prayer Book*, are too late.

The *Yoser* is without doubt an ancient prayer which derives from the temple liturgy; but the Genizah Fragments published by Schechter indicate that the prayer was originally much shorter than that of *Seder Amram Gaon*.[11] The alphabetical acrostics are almost certainly post sixth-century additions. The *Qedussah* is an ancient liturgical formula, for its context in Isaiah 6 where the prophet's vision stems from the temple worship, suggests that it was an established part of the liturgy at that date.[12] But temple usage is not the same as the synagogue; the Genizah Fragments do not contain this portion of the *Yoser*, and there is no cogent proof for the existence in Palestine of a *Qedussah* in *Yoser* in the second century A.D.[13] Similarly with the *Ahabah*; rabbinic interpretation of the temple worship given in *Mishna Tamid V* maintains that the *Ahabah* was recited every morning in the period of the second temple, but according to Finkelstein, it was quite unknown before about A.D. 150-200.[14] Again, the evidence of the Genizah Fragments indicate that the petition for peace is a later insertion.[15]

Yet in spite of this criticism, there is certainly no reason to abandon Vellian's important comparison in its more general terms. The texts of the *berakoth* were not fixed in the first or second centuries A.D., and the Genizah Fragments probably represent what was by custom usually said, and not necessarily all that was said. The omission of the *Qedussah* from the *Yoser* does not necessarily mean that it was not used. In the Apocalypse in the vision of the heavenly worship, the *Sanctus* is sung, not by the Seraphim as in Isaiah, but by the four living creatures; and it is also the "holy Chayoth," the living creatures of Ezekiel who utter the *Qedussah*. In fact, several Christian liturgies open with a preface and *Sanctus* which resemble the *Yoser* with *Qedussah* too closely to be an accident; the use of the *Sanctus* in Christian liturgy suggests an early rather than a late date for the synagogue *Qedussah*.[16] The texts of the prayers were handed down orally and were to some extend flexible and could be elaborated—for otherwise they could not have reached the present form in the modern synagogue service. A certain liberty was allowed, and themes of peace and for the gathering of Israel—themes which certainly antedate Christianity[17]—might well have been included in the second-century synagogue *berakoth*. It will be recalled that a similar freedom was enjoyed by the Christian president or bishop.[18] There is no logical reason why, in the early second century, when giving thanks, a bishop of a Jewish Christian congregation could not have modelled his eucharistic prayer on the developing synagogue *berakoth*, possibly at a time when the *synaxis* and the *missa fidelium* were becoming one service.

Indeed, we should be warned against the arbitrary reasons which scholars sometimes give for unnecessary and ruthless emendation. If similar themes are present in pre-Christian or contemporaneous Jewish liturgy, there is no valid reason for excising them from Christian liturgy. This also applies to the lack of logical sequence which again the Jewish *berakoth* display in some places; the fact that in an anaphora paragraphs do not always connect cannot be an *a priori* reason for jettisoning certain parts of them. But above all there is certainly no need to weld Addai and Mari into one short prayer with one doxology. In his assessment Ratcliff assumed that the early eucharistic prayer was always of this nature. Such an assumption is not entirely justified. The *birkat ha-mazon* which many regard as the type of prayer used by Jesus at the Last Supper in association with the cup, consisted not of one prayer with a single doxology, but of three *berakoth*, each with a doxology. A strong case has been made for the prayer in *Didache 10* being merely a Christianized version of the *birkat ha-mazon*, and this prayer also consists of three blessings each with a Chatimah.[19] Justin Martyr, remarking that the president gives thanks "at considerable length," states that "Amen" was said by the people when he had concluded "the prayers and thanksgivings."[20] The plural may not be without significance. There is no *a priori* reason why the first doxology in Addai and Mari should be regarded as an interpolation simply because it divides the anaphora into two parts. The eucharistic prayer, which is one complete prayer with a careful sequence of thought and which contains clear link words between the various sections, may well be the prayer upon which the redactor, or the Hellenizer, has been at work. Perhaps the single anaphora of the Apostolic Tradition, which has dominated twentieth-century liturgical revision, belongs in this latter category; certainly there is no reason to regard this latter as the only authentic pattern for the early eucharistic prayer.[21]

On analogy with the two synagogue *berakoth* preceding the *Shema*, it would be quite legitimate to express the structure of the *Mar Eša'ya* text as follows:

Berakah 1	(a)	Dialogue. Let your mind be on high.
	(b)	Blessing. Worthy of Glory from all mouths.
	(c)	*Sanctus*. Thousands upon Thousands.
	(d)	Anamnesis of the work of Christ. And with these heavenly hosts.
	(e)	Doxology.
Berakah 2	(f)	*Ghāntā*. In your great and unspeakable mercies.
	(g)	*Ghāntā*. So that all the inhabitants.
	(h)	(Anamnesis?). We too O Lord.
	(i)	Epiclesis.
	(j)	Doxology.

On the same analogy, there is adequate justification (though certainly not conclusive proof!) for assigning the text to the second century.

In comparing the *Mar Eša'ya* text with the *Yoser* and *Ahabah*, Vellian finds no place which explicitly invites the institution narrative.[22] Indeed, if the comparison is valid, the only place in which a narrative could come is after the two *berakoth* as a parallel with the *Shema*, as it does in the Malabar liturgy. Such a position is theologically defensible, since the words spoken by Jesus followed the blessings and were not part of them. It would also give a precedent for the position it occupies in many Reformed rites. But the evidence of the Malabar liturgy is too late to be of any value here, and in any case its position in this liturgy seems itself to be one answer to the problem of an apparent absence.

A very strong argument for the inclusion of an institution narrative within the Anaphora of Addai and Mari was put forward by Dom Bernard Botte.[23] Botte's argument centers on the prayer after the *ghāntā* for the church, (par. h) where the text he used reads thus:

> And we also, o my Lord, your weak, frail and miserable servants who are gathered together in your name, both stand before you at this time and have received the example which is from you delivered unto us, rejoicing and praising and exalting and commemorating and celebrating this great and fearful and holy and lifegiving and divine mystery of the passion and the death and the burial and the resurrection of our Lord and Savior Jesus Christ.

Botte finds a hiatus at the beginning of this paragraph, the words of which seem to require a foregoing sentence. Furthermore, the last part of the paragraph, "commemorating . . . resurrection," recalls the phraseology found in the classical anamnesis which follows the institution narrative. In another East Syrian anaphora, that of Theodore, an anamnesis is found which has similar wording to this paragraph of Addai and Mari, but there it follows an institution narrative which has a peculiar form.

> On the night when he was betrayed, with his apostles he celebrated this mystery, great, awesome, holy and divine: taking bread he blessed it and broke it and gave it to his disciples saying: this is my body which is broken for you so that sins may be forgiven.
>
> Likewise with the chalice: he offered thanks, gave it to them and said: this is the blood of the new covenant which is shed for many so that sins may be forgiven. Take, all of you, and eat of this bread and drink of this chalice, and do this whenever you gather together in memory of me.
>
> We are now gathered together just as he prescribed, we, your weak, frail and miserable servants, to celebrate by your favor the great, awesome, holy and divine mystery by which the salvation of all our human race has been accomplished.

If this institution narrative is connected with the paragraph of Addai and Mari, the words of the latter seem to echo the words from Theodore. Botte also finds a reference to the institution narrative in Ephraem and Aphrahat, where the institution narrative seems to have ended "whenever you are gathered together in my name." The paragraph of Addai and Mari would seem to follow on from such an institution narrative and may therefore be regarded as an anamnesis. The conclusion which can be drawn from this is that this anamnesis is the record of a recital of an institution narrative which has disappeared.[24]

Botte's argument is extremely convincing, though it has been questioned on two accounts. The first is the objection made by Dom H. Engberding.[25] Although accepting the paragraph as authentic, Engberding does not believe that it is an anamnesis. The difficulty is that the sentence contains no main verb, and translators and researchers have tried to discover one. Thus Renaudot makes "commemorating" and "celebrating" the main verbs; Brightman, "we stand" and "we have received"; Botte confines himself to "we have received." Engberding compares it with other anaphoras to see if similar constructions are found elsewhere. He finds similar constructions spread widely in the intercessions where after a prayer for the dead there occurs one for the living introduced by "we also." Very similar is a section in the Anaphora of Nestorius:

> Therefore, o Lord, we thy weak, frail and miserable servants, who are far from you, yet whom in the multitude of your mercies you have vouchsafed to stand before you, and minister this awful, glorious, and divine service.

The paragraph of Addai and Mari is then, according to Engberding, a continuation of the *ghāntā* for the living; it forms part of the intercessions and is not an anamnesis.

The second objection to Botte's hypothesis comes from the *Mar Eša'ya* text of Addai and Mari. Botte's argument was strengthened by the references of Ephraem and Aphrahat to a narrative which ended with the words "gathered together in my name," which Addai and Mari seems to pick up. But the *Mar Eša'ya* text does not contain the key phrase "in your name." In his consideration of the implications of the *Mar Eša'ya* text Emmanuel Cutrone believed that this greatly weakened, if not totally destroyed, Botte's argument.[26]

Let us consider the second of these objections. Though Botte's argument is weakened by the *Mar Eša'ya* text, Cutrone surely exaggerates in the suggestion that it is totally destroyed. Botte appealed to the anamnesis of Theodore, which still lends some support to his argument. A similar institution narrative-anamnesis link is to be found in the Ethiopic Anaphora of St. John the Evangelist.

> And likewise He gave praise over the cup also, and said, This cup is My Blood of the new covenant, Take drink of it, all of you. It is a wondrous sign to all who worship Him, (and) a bar of judgment to them that crucified (Him), which was written with His Blood and sealed by His Cross and signed by His death unto eternal life, by which sin is forgiven. And thus make memorial of Me when you are gathered together.
>
> We also, o Lord, who have gathered together to make memorial of your Passion and be partakers with you in your resurrection from the dead, beseech thee, o Lord our God, that as the bread was gathered when it was scattered over mountains and hills and in the desert and valleys, and being gathered was made one perfect loaf, even so gather us from every evil thought of sin into your perfect faith, and as the mingling of this wine with water cannot be separated into its two parts, even so may your Godhead be joined with our manhood and our manhood with your Godhead, your greatness with our lowliness and our lowliness with your greatness.[27]

The expansion of the words of institution and the use of the Didache in the anamnesis here suggest that the anaphora, or this part of it, is relatively late. But we give it merely to illustrate that here is another anamnesis which commences "we also" and centers on "gathered together"; there is no phrase "in your name," but it is nevertheless an anamnesis. Even without the phrase "in your name," the paragraph in *Mar Eša'ya* could still be an anamnesis. The words "in your name" may be a later refinement. There is even the possibility that they have dropped out of the *Mar Eša'ya* text.

What of Dom Engberding's objection? To accept that the paragraph is a continuation of the *ghāntā* would certainly solve the problem of the main verb, and would also exclude the necessity of an institution narrative at this point in the anaphora. However, the links with the institution narrative in Theodore make it difficult to believe that Botte is entirely mistaken in his estimation of the paragraph. As an anamnesis, it would appear to be of a primitive form; it is, for example, less developed than that of Byzantine Basil, and limits the commemoration to passion, death, burial, and resurrection. In this respect it can be compared with that of Apostolic Tradition where the commemoration is confined to *"mortis et resurrectionis."* It is so like an anamnesis that we may be forgiven for mistaking it for one. For my own part, I accept that the paragraph is an anamnesis, and presupposes an institution narrative. But this must be immediately qualified; as well as the problem of the main verb, the paragraph switches from addressing the Son to the Father, and it leaves us with a carefully constructed link with a particular form of the institution narrative. We have previously noted that where we find careful link words, the redactor may well have been hard at work.

It is at this point that we turn to consider Maronite *Sharar* or the Anaphora of St. Peter III. The close relationship that exists between Addai and Mari and sections of Maronite *Sharar* was pointed out long ago by such distinguished liturgists as Rahmani and Baumstark, and more recently by Engberding and W.F. Macomber.[28] In spite of this, *Sharar* has been ignored by most scholars, or simply dismissed without consideration. Possibly this results from a lack of confidence in a community which in the fifth century was devoted to Byzantine language, culture, and faith, and in the seventh century embraced monothelitism, and which at the time of the Crusades became a Uniate Church. Its liturgies are West Syrian with Roman importations.[29] Again, many parts of *Sharar* are late insertions such as private devotions of the celebrant. However, a careful comparison between the relevant passages of *Sharar* with the *Mar Eša'ya* text suggests that any hasty dismissal of the Maronite anaphora is extremely unwise. The relationship is such as to indicate an underlying common source; furthermore, the Maronite anaphora contains an institution narrative.

In many instances Maronite *Sharar* seems to have preserved a more original text. In Addai and Mari the opening prayer of praise is addressed to the Trinity, the post-*Sanctus* to the Son, and the *ghāntā* for the dead and the anamnesis oscillate between the Father and the Son. When the corresponding sections of *Sharar* are compared, the opening prayer of praise is also addressed to the Trinity, but from the post-*Sanctus* to the concluding doxology, the corresponding sections are addressed to the Son.

In both instances the address to the Trinity is late; the text may have originally read:

> Glory to you the adorable and glorious Name, who created the worlds through your grace and all its (their?) inhabitants through compassion. And made redemption for mortals through grace.[30]

However, was it addressed to the Father or to the Son? Which is the most likely? Would the Maronites have deliberately altered an anaphora which was addressed to the Father so as to address it to the Son? Although this is not inconsistent with monothelitism, it seems unlikely, and why should not a similar change be found in the other Maronite anaphoras? It is much more likely that *Sharar* confirms the suggestion of Ratcliff that Addai and Mari was originally addressed to the Son throughout. The East Syrian text has been altered, though since the post-*Sanctus* is applicable only to Christ, it has remained unaltered.

Sharar might also explain the position of the *Sanctus*. According to Ratcliff, the *Sanctus* in Addai and Mari is out of place.

> The clauses that introduce this have no connexion with what precedes them. They have no relevance except to the Sanctus; and the whole passage coming in between a thanksgiving for salvation and grace is out of place. As in the Roman Rite so in the East-Syrian, the Sanctus is an intrusion.[31]

Ratcliff assumed two things: first, that if the paragraph has no connection with what precedes it, it must therefore be an interpolation; and secondly, that because the *Sanctus* in the Roman rite appears to be an intrusion, it is legitimate to draw the same conclusion for Addai and Mari. But it is not necessary to arrive at such a conclusion. Addai and Mari praises God who created the world and its inhabitants; in *Sharar* Glory is offered to him who created the world and its inhabitants. Perhaps here the readings of the manuscript *Aleppensis 619* and *Monacensis 5*, "their inhabitants" is to be preferred. The *Sanctus* would then follow as an affirmation of Glory; it would be quite logical as the heavenly "Glory" offered to God from the higher world, to which is then added the thanksgiving of redeemed mortals of the lower world. Perhaps the demythologizer has been hard at work in the East Syrian text? And may it not be possible that its interpolation into the Roman Canon was precisely because there existed some anaphoras whose Jewish pedigree was such that they had always included it?

That *Sharar* has sometimes preserved the better reading is particularly notable in the post-*Sanctus* prayer.

Sharar	Addai and Mari
	And with these heavenly powers we
We give thanks to you, O Lord,	give thanks to you, O Lord, even we,
	your lowly, weak and miserable
we your sinful servants	servants, because you have effected
because you have effected in	in us a great grace which cannot be
us your grace which cannot be	repaid, in that you put on our
repaid. You put on our humanity so	humanity so as to quicken us by

as to quicken us by your divinity. You lifted up our poverty and righted our dejection. And you quickened our mortality, and you justified our sinfulness and you forgave our debts. And you enlightened our understanding, and vanquished our enemies and made triumphant our lowliness.

your divinity. And you lifted up our poor estate, and righted our fall. And you forgave us our debts. You justified our sinfulness and you enlightened our understanding. And you, our Lord and our God, vanquished our enemies and made triumphant the lowliness of our weak nature through the abounding compassion of your grace.

The Maronite version has thirty-one Syriac words compared with forty-five in *Mar Eša'ya*; twenty-eight Syriac words are common to both. Of the extra three words in *Sharar*, only one word, "sinful," is entirely new, corresponding to the *Mar Eša'ya* "weak, frail and miserable." The other two words (*ramyuthan*; *'ahith*) are synonyms for the *Mar Eša'ya* words (*mappultha*; *nahemth*). It is possible, of course, that the Maronite redactor has made a précis of the East Syrian text. But it seems fairly certain that with regard to the opening sentence of Addai and Mari, "And with these heavenly hosts," the East Syrian text has been provided with a link phrase with the *Sanctus*, which, had it been original, the Maronite redactor is unlikely to have abandoned.

Another example is the epiclesis.

Sharar

Addai and Mari

Hear me, O Lord. Hear me, O Lord. Hear me, O Lord. And may he come, O Lord, your living and Holy Spirit, and dwell and rest upon this oblation of your servants. And may it be to those who partake for the pardon of debts and the forgiveness of sins and for a blessed resurrection from the dead and a new life in the kingdom of heaven for ever.

May he come, O Lord, your Holy Spirit and rest upon this oblation of your servants, and bless and hallow it, that it may be to us, O Lord, for the pardon of debts and the forgiveness of sins, and a great hope of resurrection from the dead and a new life in the kingdom of heaven with all who have been pleasing before you.

Here it would appear that Addai and Mari have been interpolated by "bless it and hallow it" from the other two Nestorian anaphoras, Theodore and Nestorius.[32] Again, it is difficult to believe that the Maronite redactor carefully removed these words when they occur in his institution narrative.

Although not every section is so favorable to *Sharar*, there is sufficient reason for taking this anaphora very seriously in any estimation of the *Mar Eša'ya* text. This includes the institution narrative of the Maronite anaphora; could the "missing" institution narrative of Addai and Mari be that of *Sharar*?

The institution narrative in *Sharar* is indeed unusual, both in its position and its form. It comes after the *ghāntā* for the righteous fathers and precedes a lengthy anamnesis and intercession which contains the *ghāntā* for the church. The text is addressed to the Son:

> We make, O Lord, the memorial of your passion as you have taught us: In that night when you were delivered up to the crucifiers, O Lord, you took bread in your pure and holy hands, and you looked up to heaven to your glorious Father. You blessed, and signed, hallowed, O Lord, and broke and gave to your disciples, the blessed apostles, and said to them, 'This bread is my body which is broken and given for the life of the world, and for those who take it, for the pardon of debts and forgiveness of sins. Take, eat from it, and it will be to you for eternal life'.

> *And he takes the cup and says:*

> And likewise over the cup you gave thanks and glorified and said, O Lord, 'This cup is my blood of the New Testament which is shed for many for the remission of sins. Take, drink from it all of you, and it will be to you for the pardon of debts and forgiveness of sins and eternal life'. Amen.

> *And he says:*

> For whenever you eat from this holy body and drink from this cup of life and salvation you are calling to remembrance the death and resurrection of your Lord until the great day of his coming.

This institution account has been the subject of consideration by A. Raes and W.F. Macomber.[33] Raes, noting the strange form, "This bread is my body," which provides a parallel with the cup saying, and also the characteristic West Syrian phrase "remission of sins and life eternal," concluded that it showed signs of decadence, and could not therefore be original.[34] Macomber, however, was prepared to accept that *Sharar* may well have preserved for us both the location and the substance of the original narrative of the Anaphora of the Apostles.[35] The positioning of the institution is so unusual as to suggest that it is original; a redactor is unlikely to have composed an institution narrative addressed to the Son, a feature which has a parallel in some of the Ethiopic anaphoras. Furthermore, although there is the strange form of the bread saying, Macomber notes that overall there is a lack of symmetry, which often indicates an early date.

Of these two considerations and opinions, Raes would seem to be on firmer ground. Diversity of forms of the institution narrative is a feature of West Syrian anaphoras, and not all forms which lack symmetry are of an early date.[36] The fact that the institution is addressed to the Son again is not necessarily primitive, but rather a sign that the Maronite redactor has been consistent; it would have been odd indeed for the institution to be addressed to the Father when it succeeds a number of paragraphs addressed to the Son.

The position of the narrative also suggests that it is a later addition. The writer knows of no other institution narrative that follows a commemoration of the dead. Furthermore, if the commemoration of the righteous fathers is compared with that of Addai and Mari, it would appear that here the East Syrian text is preferable. Whereas the *Mar Eša'ya* text continues with a prayer for peace and then with the *ghāntā* for the church, in *Sharar* the *ghāntā* for the righteous fathers suddenly develops into a quotation from John 6:1: "'I am the bread of life which came down from heaven' so that mortals may have life through me." Yet one of the characteristics of Addai and Mari is its lack of direct reference to the New Testament. Furthermore, the narrative has a pick-up on the words "you have taught us," which might suggest the hand of the refiner.

However, the two most important factors against this narrative in *Sharar* being the "missing" narrative of Addai and Mari are, first, it simply is not in Addai and Mari, and, second, it does not have the correct form to connect with the anamnesis of the East Syrian text. *Sharar* has its own anamnesis embedded in the intercessions. It is quite different from that of Addai and Mari.

But if *Sharar* is of little help in the quest to supply an institution narrative for Addai and Mari, it is important in the question of the authenticity of the latter's anamnesis paragraph. This paragraph which has no main verb, is perhaps the most problematical section of Addai and Mari. The whole paragraph is absent from *Sharar*, and this must raise a question regarding its date. Perhaps it could be a later insertion by the East Syrian redactor, and this possibility is increased by the fact that parallels are found in Theodore and Nestorius, with these latter perhaps being the source of the interpolation. On the other hand, many scholars have regarded this section as having a primitive "ring" to it. The words "received by tradition the example (model) which is from you" are clearly a reference to the institution of the eucharist, and one might speculate as to whether there is some connection here with 1 Corinthians 11:23 where, underlying Paul's Greek, the rabbinical terms *qibbel* ("received") and *masar* ("delivered") are used to introduce the institution. Perhaps the best explanation is that this "anamnesis" paragraph is better termed a primitive Syrian "institution-anamnesis," dating from a time when a reference to the institution or the Lord's example was regarded as quite adequate. If this is the case, then the Maronite redactor, or developing tradition, came to regard them as inadequate, and so removed the paragraph, replacing it with a full institution narrative and anamnesis.

In conclusion, it is possible to see Addai and Mari as a prayer with a bipartite structure, or two -*berakoth* structure. The first glorifies the Name (of Christ) with the *Sanctus*, post-*Sanctus*, and doxology, which has Jewish parallels.[37] The second consisted of a commemoration of the righteous fathers, a plea for peace, and prayer for the *ecclesia*, a reference to the example of Christ, an epiclesis, and doxology. In this form it came before the Maronite redactor who included a full institution narrative and anamnesis in place of the older "institution-anamnesis."

Notes

1. Bayard H. Jones, "The History of the Nestorian Liturgies," *Anglican Theological Review* 46 (1964) 155-176, particularly 174.

2. For example, G. Dix, *The Shape of the Liturgy* (London: Dacre Press, Adam and Charles Black, 1945); B. Botte, "L'anaphore chaldéenne des apôtres," *Orientalia Christiana Periodica* 15 (1949) 259-276; L. Bouyer, *Eucharist*, tr. C.U. Quinn (Notre Dame: University of Notre Dame Press, 1968); L. Ligier, "From the Last Supper to the Eucharist," in *The New Liturgy*, ed. Lancelot Sheppard (London: Darton, Longmann and Todd Limited, 1970).

3. R.H. Connolly, E. Bishop, "The Work of Menezes on the Malabar Liturgy," *Journal of Theological Studies* 15 (1914) 396-425, 569-589; F.C. Burkitt, "The Old Malabar Liturgy," *Journal of Theological Studies* 29 (1928) 155-157.

4. *Vat. cod. syr. 66* of Mar Joseph, Metropolitan of Malabar (d. 1569) gives the words of institution with their setting on a separate page at the beginning of the liturgy, with a note that they are to be recited probably after the fraction and consignation; in both the Menezian and Rozian liturgies, the position is after the anaphora and before the fraction. Placid of S. Joseph, "The Present Syro-Malabar Liturgy: Menezian or Rozian?" *Orientalia Christiana Periodica* 23 (1957) 313-331.

5. W.F. Macomber, "The Oldest Known Text of the Anaphora of the Apostles Addai and Mari," *Orientalia Christiana Periodica* 32 (1966) 335-371.

6. E.C. Ratcliff, "The Original Form of the Anaphora of Addai and Mari: A Suggestion," *Journal of Theological Studies* 30 (1928-1929) 23-32.

7. Ibid. 27.

8. Ibid. 29.

9. Ibid. 30ff.

10 J. Vellian, "The Anaphoral Structure of Addai and Mari Compared to the Berakoth Preceding the Shema in the Synagogue Morning Service Contained in Seder R. Amram Gaon," *Le Muséon* 85 (1972) 201-223.

11. S. Schechter, "Genizah Specimens," *The Jewish Quarterly Review* 10 (1898) 654-659; Jacob Mann, "Genizah Fragments of the Palestinian Order of Service," *Hebrew Union College Annual* 2 (1925) 269-338; W.O.E. Oesterley, *The Jewish Background of the Christian Liturgy* (Oxford: Oxford University Press, 1925) 48-49.

12 Otto Kaiser, *Isaiah 1-12* (London: SCM, 1972) 76; J. Bright, "Isaiah - I," in *Peake's Commentary on the Bible*, ed. M. Black and H.H. Rowley (London: Nelson, 1962).

13. Mann, "Genizah Fragments."

14. Quoted in C.W. Dugmore, *The Influence of the Synagogue upon the Divine Office* (London: Faith Press, 1964) 21.

15. Schechter, "Genizah Spcimens" 655.

16. C.P. Price, "Jewish Morning Prayers and Early Christian Anaphoras," *Anglican Theological Review* 43 (1961) 153-168.

17. See, for example, the Palestinian text of the *Amidah*, Benedictions 14 and 18, which Dugmore, *The Influence of the Synagogue*, dates 168 B.C. and 40-70 A.D. respectively.

18. R.P.C. Hanson, "The Liberty of the Bishop to Improvise Prayer in the Eucharist." *Vigiliae Christianae* 15 (1961) 173-175.

19. L. Finkelstein, "The Birkat Ha-Mazon," *Jewish Quarterly Review*, New Series 19 (1928) 211ff.

20. Apology I, 67.

21. See J.P. Audet, "Literary Forms and Contents of a Normal Eucharistia in the First Century," in *Texte und Untersuchungen* 73 (1959), ed. K. Aland and others, 661: "the consequences due to the psychological implantation of the old eucharistia in a community henceforth almost exclusively made up of human elements drawn from the Gentile world, becoming perceptible as early as the end of the second century. At the beginning of the third, where the Apostolic Tradition of Hippolytus can be dated, we get a strong impression that things have changed rapidly. What was henceforth beginning to take place, was roughly some kind of an inner breaking and dissociation of the literary forms of the ancient eucharistia, together with corresponding modifications in the balance of the significations and values which the eucharistia had originally been intended to serve."

22. Vellian, "The Anaphoral Structure" 217. In his critical edition of the *Mar Eša'ya* text, William Macomber ("The Oldest Known Text") does not commit himself on the question: "Nor should it cause any surprise that there is no Narration of the institution of the Eucharist in the *Mar Eša'ya* text, as its loss if indeed it ever did exist in the Anaphora of the Apostles, must go back at least to the abbreviation effected by Iso'yabh III in the seventh century" (348-349).

23. B. Botte, "L'anaphore chaldéenne des apôtres"; Botte, "Problèmes de l'anaphore syrienne des apôtres Addaï et Mari," *L'Orient syrien* 10 (1965) 89-106.

24. Botte, "Problemes" 103.

25. H. Engberding, "Zum anaphorischen Fürbittgebet der ostsyrischen Liturgie der Apostel Addaj und Mar (j)," *Oriens Christianus* 41 (1957) 102-124, esp. 113f.

26. E.J. Cutrone, "The Anaphora of the Apostles: Implications of the *Mar Eša'ya* Text," *Theological Studies* 43 (1973) 624ff, p. 639. Cutrone appears to be unaware of Vellian's assessment.

27. J.M. Harding, *The Anaphoras of the Ethiopic Liturgy* (London: SPCK, 1928) 81.

28. I.E. Rahmani, *Testamentum Domini Nostri Jesu Christi* (Moguntiae, 1899); A. Baumstark, "Altlibanesische Liturgie," *Oriens Christianus* 4 (1904) 190-194; H. Engberding, "Urgestalt, Eingenart und Entwicklung eines altantiochenischen eucharistischen Hochgebetes," *Oriens Christianus* 29 (1932) 32-48; W.F. Macomber, "The Maronite and Chaldean Versions of the Anaphora of the Apostles," *Orientalia Christiana Periodica* 37 (1971) 55-84.

29. Archdale A. King, *The Rites of Eastern Christendom*, 2 volumes (Rome: Catholic Book Agency, 1947) vol. 1, chapter 3.

30. The Syriac text used here is that of J.M. Sauget in *Anaphorae Syriacae*, vol. 2, Fasciculus 3 (Rome: Pontificium Institutum Orientalium Studiorum, 1973).

31. E.C. Ratcliff, "The Original Form" 29.

32. See B. Botte, "L'épiclèse dans les liturgies syriennes orientales," *Sacris Eruditi* 6 (1954) 48-72.

33. A. Raes, "Le récit de l'institution eucharistique dans l'anaphore chaldéenne et malabare des apôtres," *Orientalia Christiana Periodica* 10 (1944) 216-226; W.F. Macomber, "The Maronite and Chaldean Versions."

34. Raes, "Le récit de l'institution" 223.

35. Macomber, "The Maronite and Chaldean Versions" 72.

36. A. Raes, "Les paroles de la consécration dans les anaphores syriennes," *Orientalia Christiana Periodica* 3 (1937) 486-504. See also the strange form in the Ethiopic Liturgies.

37. See the *berakoth* from *Ma'aseh Merkavah*, in Bryan D. Spinks, *The Sanctus in the Eucharistic Prayer* (Cambridge: Cambridge University Press, 1991).

3

Addai and Mari and the Institution Narrative: The Tantalizing Evidence of Gabriel Qatraya

THE COMMENTARY ON THE NESTORIAN LITURGICAL RITES BY GABRIEL QATRAYA Bar Lip(h)ah is found in the British Museum's thirteenth-century manuscript *Or. 3336*, and is apparently the only surviving copy.[1] Although mentioned in a footnote by Anton Baumstark,[2] it is due to the work of S.H. Jammo that it has been brought to the attention of liturgical scholars.[3] According to Jammo, Qatraya's work is to be dated between 615-625 A.D. Towards the conclusion of his article in *Orientalia Christiana Periodica* Jammo wrote:

> La présence ou l'absence de la narration de la Cène du Seigneur dans l'anaphore d'Addaï et Mari a suscité déja bien études dont la dernière est celle de B. Botte. Le nouveau texte pourrait-il apporter quelque lumière dans cet épineux problème?[4]

This short note is concerned to consider the *"lumière"* which this manuscript brings to the *"épineux problème."*

RECENT VIEWS ON ADDAI AND MARI AND THE INSTITUTION NARRATIVE

To date the solutions which have been offered to the apparent absence of an institution narrative in Addai and Mari fall into three distinct categories.

1.   The position of older scholars such as Edward Ratcliff and Gregory Dix was that the anaphora had never contained an institution narrative. Ratcliff, perhaps with Lietzmann's "two-types" of early eucharist in mind, preferred to see Addai and Mari as a *eucharistia* rather than as an anaphora.[5] Dix was also of the opinion that Addai and Mari never had a narrative of the institution.[6]

2.   Scholars such as Raes, Dalmais, Botte, and Bouyer, have argued in different ways that the anaphora did originally have an institution narrative, but it was not, or is no longer, found in the manuscript tradition. According to Raes and Dalmais,[7] the institution narrative was recited from memory, and on account of the *disciplina arcani*, was not written in the text. A very ingenious and convincing argument was put forward by Bernard Botte.[8] By comparing Addai and Mari with the Anaphora of Theodore, Botte argued that the paragraph "And we also, O Lord—*thrice*—your lowly, weak and miserable servants who was gathered together (in your name) and stand before you at this time, etc." (Paragraph G of my English edition of the *Mar Eša'ya* anaphora[9]), is in fact an anamnesis marking the place where there had been an institution narrative. He noted the peculiar form of the narrative in Theodore ending with the words "Be doing thus whenever you gather together in my memory."[10] In Aphrahat and Ephraem he found references to the institution narrative ending in similar words. He concluded that the "anamnesis"" of Addai and Mari is the record of an institution narrative which has since disappeared, and that this narrative ended with the words "Be doing thus whenever you gather together in my memory," or "Be doing thus whenever you gather together in my name," an East Syrian peculiarity. Botte's position has been supported by Louis Bouyer.[11] The view that an institution narrative has at some stage dropped out of the text claims support also from a reference of Abulfaraj Ibn-at-Tayyib (+ 1043):

> The Quddasha of the Apostles was composed by Addai and Mari; and the Catholicos Isho'yabh of Adiabene abridged it.[12]

This is taken to be a reference to an abridgement made by Ishoyabh III (?648-658), and it is surmised that he removed the narrative.

3.   Since the publication of J.M. Sauget's text of the Maronite anaphora called *Sharar*, a number of more recent studies have been concerned to reconstruct the "original" text of the Anaphora of the Apostles underlying *Sharar* and Addai and Mari. Even before Sauget's publication, William Macomber pointed out that the Maronite anaphora contained an institution narrative which was addressed to

the Son, and had certain peculiar characteristics.[13] He suggested that *Sharar* may well have preserved both the location and the form of the "missing" institution narrative now absent from Addai and Mari. In his recent reconstruction of the "common" Syriac text, c. 400 A.D., Macomber has included *Sharar's* narrative.[14] José Manuel Sánchez Caro and, although allowing it to be a secondary development of the anaphora, H. Wegman, also regard *Sharar's* narrative as the missing narrative of Addai and Mari.[15] Isho-yabh III is again held responsible for its suppression in Addai and Mari.

Since Gabriel Qatraya's commentary pre-dates the abridgement attributed to Isho-yabh III, any information about an institution narrative which can be shown to have been cited or mentioned in connection with Addai and Mari rather than with the anaphoras of Theodore or Nestorius, would have considerable implications for the views outlined above.

QATRAYA AND THE INSTITUTION NARRATIVE AS AN ESSENTIAL PART OF CONSECRATION

S.H. Jammo drew attention to the fact that Qatraya emphasizes the importance of the recitation by the priest of the words of Christ at the Last Supper. He published the Syriac text and Latin translation of ff. 199r-200r, which contains that section of the commentary dealing with the anaphora.[16] Jammo compared Qatraya's comments with those of other Nestorian commentators—Abraham Bar Lip(h)ah, Yohannan Bar Zo'bi, who both supported Qatraya's theology of consecration, Mar Abdiso and Pseudo-George Arbela, who play down or pass over the institution narrative in favor of the epiclesis. This particular reference of Qatraya, in his comments on the anaphora, indicates that this Nestorian commentator knew that an institution narrative was recited, and that it was important for consecration.

Jammo's survey has been repeated and expanded slightly by Edward Kilmartin.[17] Kilmartin draws attention to ff. 204r-204v, where Qatraya appeals to Genesis 1:28, arguing that like that blessing, that by which the Lord blessed bread and wine perdures to eternity and will not cease.[18] Noting the striking parallels in Chrysostom's *De Proditione Judae Homilia* 1,6, Kilmartin suggests that quite possibly Qatraya derived his theology of consecration from Chrysostom's homily.[19]

Both Jammo and Kilmartin are mainly concerned with Qatraya's ideas about consecration, and it is clear that he regarded both the words of institution and the epiclesis as necessary for consecration.

Since Addai and Mari is the most used anaphora, it may be inferred that Qatraya is commenting on this anaphora, and therefore in his day it included words of institution. Certainly Jammo infers this.[20] However, the commentary on the anaphora is so brief and so general that Qatraya could easily be commenting on the East Syrian anaphoras in general, or have in mind Theodore or Nestorius. There is no obvious quotation which helps us. The verb he uses with reference to the epiclesis, *gn*, overshadow, occurs only in Theodore (*thagen*), but Qatraya seems to be giving a general theological explanation of the function of the epiclesis rather than alluding to the epiclesis of a particular anaphora. The commentary is so general that it could serve for practically any anaphora. The reference to the narrative of institution on f. 199r is so brief and its context so general that it is of little help in tackling the enigma of Addai and Mari.

QATRAYA'S TANTALIZING EVIDENCE

Jammo and Kilmartin confined their investigation to that part of the commentary which deals with the anaphora. However, at two points earlier in the commentary on the eucharist, Qatraya refers to the institution narrative, and gives a fuller quotation than his brief mention on f. 199r.

1. f. 184 recto

> And this the Apostle says as the Word of our Lord which he said in the delivering of the mysteries "before he suffered, taking bread in his holy hands, he blessed and broke and gave to his disciples and said: 'This is my body which is broken for you for the forgiveness of sins'. And also over the cup he gave thanks and gave it to them and said: 'This is my blood of the new covenant which is shed for many for the forgiveness of sins'." And he added more and said "Be doing thus whenever you gather together in my memory."

2. f. 196 verso

> But bread and wine he blessed and broke and gave to them and said: "This is my body" and "This is my blood. Take, eat and drink from it all of you, and be doing thus whenever you gather together in my memory."

These two references, simply because they are not given in the context of comments on the anaphora, must be used with caution. However, they raise a number of interesting points.

A comparison of the narrative on f. 184r with that of the Anaphora of Theodore reveals that it could be dependent upon the narrative of that anaphora. We give the narrative from Theodore with common words italicized:

> Who with his holy Apostles in that night in which he was betrayed, he performed this great and fearful and holy and divine mystery, *taking bread into his holy hands*. And *he blessed and broke, and gave to his disciples and said: "This is my body which is broken* for the life of the world *for the remission of sins." And* likewise *also over the cup he gave thanks and gave it to them and said: "This is my blood of the new covenant which is shed for many for the forgiveness of sins*. Take all of you therefore; eat from this bread and drink from this cup. And *be doing thus whenever you gather together in my memory."*

The narrative of f. 196v is, of course, a short summary, but interestingly, like that of f. 184r and Theodore, it includes the words "Be doing thus, whenever you gather together (*d-methkanšin*) in my memory."[21] These words formed an important part of Botte's discussion of an institution narrative in Addai and Mari, drawing attention to the peculiarity of the words "whenever you gather together." Dom H. Engberding pointed out that this was not unique to East Syria, for it occurs in three West Syrian anaphoras, and in the Ethiopic Anaphora of St. John the Evangelist.[22] The latter appears to be a relatively late Ethiopic composition, based on foreign sources, and Syria may well be the source.[23] It is extremely difficult to date West Syrian anaphoras, and its occurrence in St. Peter I, Johannes Bar Madani and Ignatius Bar Wahib,[24] would seem to suggest that their authors were aware of some tradition or precedent for attributing these words to Jesus. Botte, it will be recalled, found an early precedent in Aphrahat:

> After Judas had gone out from their presence, he took bread and blessed and gave it to his disciples and said to them: "This is my body. Take and eat from it all of you." And over the wine in the same way he blessed and said to them: "This is my blood of the new covenant which is shed for many for the forgiveness of sins. Be doing thus in my memory when you gather together (*d-methkanšiyn*)."[25]

Exactly how or why this should have been added to the institution narrative is difficult to explain, for although it is not against the spirit of Scripture, it is not scriptural. In the *Peshitta* New Testament the verb *knš* is used to translate συνάγω (including Matthew 18:20—

gather together in my name); συναθροίζω—Luke 24:33, for the gathering in the Upper Room; and, significantly, the Ethpe'el plural participle *methkanšīn* translates συνέρχομαι at 1 Corinthians 11:18, 20, and 33. The verb is used to describe the assembling of the church (Acts 16:6, 14:27; 20:7; 1 Cor 14:23) and perhaps was in some quarters regarded as a technical word for the coming together of the eucharistic church. Whether the occurrence of *methkanšīn* surrounding the Pauline narrative in the *Peshitta* suggested it, or whether the latter itself reflects an established usage seems a matter for conjecture. It does seem to be used in a technical sense by Ephraem, who paraphrases the words over the cup thus:

> This is my true blood which is shed for all of you. Take, drink from it all of you, which is the new covenant in my blood. And as you have seen me [do], be doing thus in my memory. And lo, when you gather together (*d-methkanšīn*) in my name at church in every place perform that which I have done in my memory.[26]

In any case, its occurrence pre-dates the Anaphora of Theodore.

It may well be that on f. 184r, Qatraya was simply giving a précis of the narrative of Theodore. Elsewhere in the commentary he quotes Theodore of Mopsuestia, the father of Nestorianism, and he may well have regarded the Anaphora of Theodore to be by him, and made it the basis of his commentary.[27] But, as Douglas Webb has pointed out in a paper on the Anaphora of Theodore, although this anaphora seems to have been translated from a Greek original, and combines elements of the anaphoras of Nestorius and Addai and Mari, it seems to be no slavish translation, and tried to retain some elements of the East Syrian tradition. Webb writes:

> I will content myself with remarking that while it is undoubtedly true that some of the material in the Anaphora of Theodore is derived from the Anaphora of Nestorius, quite clearly the narrative of institution is not dependent upon that source. One could indeed go further, and point out that it is unlike the narrative of institution in any existing anaphora. It is not an unreasonable suggestion, therefore, that if indeed there ever was a narrative of institution in the Anaphora of Addai and Mari, it was couched in somewhat similar terms.[28]

It is fairly clear that with the remarks of Bernard Botte and Douglas Webb, we have too many unknowns and possibilities, and a circular argument. Even so, the question must be asked: Is it possible that Qatraya's narrative is that of Addai and Mari?

There is one small piece of tantalizing evidence. After the narrative of f. 184r, Qatraya continues (and on f. 185v):

> But if the mysteries are performed in memory *of the passion, and death and resurrection of our Lord*, the holy Apostles have correctly ordered us that everyday if possible we should not taste anything until we receive the holy mysteries, as they also were doing in their fellowship in the upper room as it is written: "They persevered in prayer and in the breaking of the eucharist."

The words "memory of the passion, death and burial and resurrection" occur in a pre-anaphoral prayer in Theodore and Nestorius, and Qatraya may well have been drawing upon this formula. However, the words also recall the type of anamnesis found after the narrative of institution in Apostolic Tradition, Apostolic Constitutions VIII, St. Basil, and St. James. No such corresponding phrases occur in the anamnesis of Theodore or Nestorius; but the words do occur in the "anamnesis" of Addai and Mari.

> And we also, O Lord—(thrice)—your lowly, weak and miserable servants who are gathered together and stand before you at this time have received by tradition of the example which is from you rejoicing, and glorifying, and magnifying, and commemorating and praising, and performing this great and dread mystery *of the passion and death and resurrection of our Lord* Jesus Christ.

It is tempting to suggest that here Qatraya is in fact referring to the anamnesis of Addai and Mari, and has preserved also the greater part of its institution narrative. The narrative he quotes is liturgical, not a biblical quotation, and so it would be logical for him to pick up words from the next part of the anaphora, the anamnesis. If we could be certain about this, then, while not proving that Addai and Mari had always had an institution narrative, it would show that in Qatraya's day there was a narrative, and that it was of the type suggested by Botte and preserved in part in Theodore, and not that found in *Sharar*. However, the evidence is tantalizing. While the context invites reference to an anamnesis, Qatraya is not at this point discussing the anaphora, and so the context does not demand such a reference. Our conclusion must be, therefore, that the evidence Qatraya brings to bear on the question of Addai and Mari and the institution narrative is tantalizingly suggestive, but remains inconclusive.

Notes

1. I am grateful to the Reverend Douglas Webb for the use of his microfilm of the manuscript.

2. A. Baumstark, *Geschichte der syrischen Literatur mit Ausschluss der Christlich palästinensischen Texte* (Bonn: A. Marcus und E. Webers Verlag, 1922) 200, note 13.

3. S. Hermiz Jammo, "Gabriel Qatraya et son commentaire sur la liturgie chaldéenne," *Orientalia Christiana Periodica* 32 (1966) 39-52; Jammo, *La Structure de la messe chaldéenne du début jusqu'à l'anaphore: Etude historique*, Orientalia Christiana Analecta, vol. 207 (Rome: Pontificium Institutum Orientalium Studiorum, 1979) 29-48.

4. Jammo, "Gabriel Qatraya et son commentaire" 52.

5. E.C. Ratcliff, "The Original Form of the Anaphora of Addai and Mari: A Suggestion," *Journal of Theological Studies* 30 (1928-1929) 23-32.

6. G. Dix, *The Shape of the Liturgy* (London: Dacre Press, Adam and Charles Black, 1945) 178ff,

7. A. Raes, "Le récit de l'institution eucharistique dans l'anaphore chaldéenne et malabare des apôtres," *Orientalia Christiana Periodica* 10 (1940) 216-226; I.-H. Dalmais, *Eastern Liturgies* (New York: Hawthorne Books, 1960) 90. Raes is less certain in "The Enigma of the Chaldean and Malabar Anaphora of the Apostles," in J. Vellian, ed., *The Malabar Church*, Orientalia Christiana Analecta (Rome: Pontificium Institutum Orientalium Studiorum, 1970) 1-8.

8. B. Botte, "L'anaphore chaldéenne des apôtres," *Orientalia Christiana Periodica* 15 (1949) 259-276; Botte, "Problèmes de l'anaphore syrienne des apôtres Addaï et Mari," *L'Orient Syrien* 10 (1965) 89-106.

9. Bryan D. Spinks, *Addai and Mari - The Anaphora of the Apostles: A Text for Students*, Grove Liturgical Study, vol. 24 (Bramcote: Grove Books, 1980). The words "in your name" are not in the *Mar Eša'ya* text, but are in all other manuscripts.

10. I have used the Urmiah edition and the *Mar Eša'ya* text of Theodore.

11. L. Bouyer, *Eucharist*, tr. C.U. Quinn (Notre Dame: University of Notre Dame Press, 1968) 147-158.

12. W. Hoenerbach and O. Spies, *Ibn At-Tayyib Fiqh An-Narsraniya*, Corpus Scriptorum Christianorum Orientalium, vol. 168 (Louvain: L. Durbecq, 1956/1957) 93.

13. W.F. Macomber, "The Maronite and Chaldean Versions of the Anaphora of the Apostles," *Orientalia Christiana Periodica* 37 (1971) 55-84.

14. Macomber, "The Ancient Form of the Anaphora of the Apostles," in *East of Byzantium: Syria and Armenia in the Formative Period*, ed. N.G. Garsoian, T.F. Mathews, and R.W. Thomson (Washington, D.C.: Dumbarton Oaks Center for Byzantine Studies, 1982).

15. J.M. Sánchez Caro, "La anfora de Addai y Mari y la anfora maronita Sarrar: intento de reconstrucción de la fuente primitiva común," *Orientalia Christiana Periodica* 43 (1977) 41-69; H.A.J. Wegman, "Pleidooi voor een Tekst de Anaphora van de Apostelen Addai en Mari," *Bijdragen* 40 (1979) 15-43

16. Jammo, "Gabriel Qatraya et son commentaire."

17. Edward J. Kilmartin, "John Chrysostom's Influence on Gabriel Qatraya's Theology of Eucharistic Consecration," *Theological Studies* 42 (1981) 444-457.

18. Ibid.

19. Ibid. Kilmartin notes that during the period that Qatraya was at Nisibis, Henānā was director, and he preferred Chrysostom's exegetical work to that of Theodore of Mopsuestia. A. Vööbus, *History of the School of Nisibis*, Corpus Scriptorum Christianorum Orientalium Subsidia, vol. 26 (Louvain: Secréteriat du Corpus SCO, 1965) 244.

20. Jammo, "Gabriel Qatraya et son commentaire" 52.

21. In fact Qatraya has attached the pronoun to the participle, giving *d-methkanšintun*, but the translation is the same.

22. H. Engberding, "Zum anaphorischen Fürbittgebet der Ostsyrischen Liturgie der Apostel Addaj und Mar(j)," *Oriens Christianus* 41 (1957) 102-124.

23. See Ernst Hammerschmidt, *Studies in the Ethiopic Anaphoras* (Berlin: Akademie-Verlag, 1961). After his detailed discussion of the anaphoras of this tradition, Hammerschmidt was unable to offer any dating.

24. E. Renaudot, *Liturgiarum Orientalium Collectio*, vol. 2 (Farnborough: Gregg International Reprint, 1970) 147, 511, 527.

25. W. Wright, *The Homilies of Aphraates*, vol. 1, *The Syriac Text* (London, 1869) 221.

26. T.J. Lamy, *Sancti Ephraem Syri, Hymni et Sermones*, vol. 1 (Mechliniae, 1882) cols. 423 and 435 (Syriac).

27. It is highly unlikely that the anaphora has anything to do with Theodore of Mopsuestia other than the name. B. Botte, "Les anaphores syriennes orientales," in *Eucharisties d'orient et d'occident*, vol. 2 (Paris: Editions du Cerf, 1970); see also the note below.

28. Douglas Webb, "The Anaphora of Theodore the Interpreter." A paper delivered to the Society for Liturgical Study, September 1981; *Ephemerides Liturgicae* 104 (1990) 3-22.

4

The East Syrian Anaphora of Theodore: Its Sources and Theology

IN MARKED CONTRAST WITH ADDAI AND MARI, THE EAST SYRIAN ANAPHORAS of Theodore and Nestorius have received only minor consideration from liturgists in recent years. There are notable exceptions. A paper by Bernard Botte, given to the liturgical week at St. Serge, which examined both anaphoras, was published in 1970;[1] and Georg Wagner also gave them some attention in his 1973 study of the Anaphora of St. John Chrysostom.[2] The Anaphora of Theodore formed the subject of a paper given by Douglas Webb to the Society for Liturgical Study in 1981, where the theme was "Liturgy, Theology and Culture."[3] However, after a lengthy background introduction, Webb's treatment was limited to a description of the anaphora to show some of the distinctive East Syrian spirit. In an article in *Orientalia Christiana Periodica* (1984) I considered the sacrificial terminology of the East Syrian anaphoras, and there made some suggestions regarding the origin and structure of both Nestorius and Theodore.[4]

In this present study it is my purpose to explore more fully the suggestion made in *Orientalia Christiana Periodica* in relation to the sources underlying the Anaphora of Theodore, together with the Christology and soteriology which seem integral to this eucharistic prayer.

THEORIES AS TO THE ORIGIN OF THE
ANAPHORA OF THEODORE

According to Leontius of Byzantium, Theodore of Mopsuestia was the author of an anaphora (blasphemous in the view of Leontius),[5] and it has been thought by some that the East Syrian anaphora is a Syriac translation of that prayer. F.E. Brightman, in an article in 1930, tried to demonstrate from the extant writings of Theodore of Mopsuestia that the anaphora reflects the stock of his vocabulary and his theological expression.[6] Brightman worked without reference to the Catechetical Lectures of Theodore, some of which Mingana was to publish in 1933.[7] The lectures were probably given when Theodore was a bishop. Although the anaphora presupposed in the Catechetical Lectures has some affinities with the East Syrian eucharistic prayer, there are also marked contrasts—not least the place of the intercessions in relation to the epiclesis. Theodore commented on an anaphora which was clearly Syro-Byzantine in structure. Botte therefore, although noting the convergences and divergences between the Catechetical Lectures and Theodore,[8] concluded that Theodore is not the anaphora which is at the base of the Lectures. Since there is a tradition that the anaphoras of Nestorius and Theodore were the work of translation by Mar Abbas after visiting Constantinople,[9] Botte was prepared to accept that Mar Abbas may have found traces of an anaphora by Theodore, and incorporated these into the Anaphora of Theodore.[10]

Georg Wagner was much more confident about the link between the Catechetical Lectures and the Anaphora of Theodore. In his much wider study, he explored three questions:[11]

1.   Was Theodore only later adapted to the East Syrian anaphoral pattern?

2.   What is the relationship between Theodore and the anaphora described in the Catechetical Lectures?

3.   What is the significance of the similarities between Theodore and the Greek Chrysostom?

Wagner noted the problem of the fact that the Catechetical Lectures presupposed a Syro-Byzantine type of anaphora, and argued that the intercessory introduction to the epiclesis of Theodore witnesses to a later dislocation, with the seam still showing.[12] He thus implies that Theodore was originally of the Syro-Byzantine pattern— and the subject of the Catechetical Lectures—and has been deliberately restructured. From this Wagner is then able to make more of the apparent parallels between the Catechetical Lecture and Theodore.[13] Finally Wagner noted how many parts of the Catechetical Lectures are compatible with the Greek Anaphora of Chrysostom (e.g., the trinitarian opening, and the post-*Sanctus*), making it possible that both formulas originated in the same area.[14]

Before proceeding further, it is necessary at this stage to question Wagner's belief that a version of Theodore underlines the Catechetical Lectures. The anaphora underlying the latter has been the subject of discussion by E. Mazza, who suggests that there is a distinction in the Catechetical Lectures between what the Ordo prescribes, and the anaphora described by the actual catecheses.[15] Mazza also makes much of the virtual absence of quotation of an institution narrative within the anaphora, concluding that Theodore knew of an anaphora which, like Addai and Mari, contained only a reference to the institution narrative.

One of the problems with Mazza's very provocative discussion is that he makes far too little allowance for the homiletic style of a catechesis, which does not always yield the accuracy which twentieth-century scholarship demands. It may be that Mazza has taken the material too much at face value.

Perhaps underneath the Catechetical Lectures there is an anaphora which Theodore composed for use at Mopsuestia. However, it could be the case that Leontius was misled, and simply assumed that since the Nestorians had an anaphora named after Theodore, it must have been his composition. Allowing for the homiletic style, Wagner was correct to note the similarities between the Catechetical Lectures and the Greek Anaphora of St. John Chrysostom—particularly in the opening praise, *Sanctus*, and immediate post-*Sanctus*. On the other hand, Mazza notes the similarities of the Christological section through to the epiclesis with Byzantine Basil.[16] It is possible that Theodore was commenting on an anaphora he had composed which drew on both these anaphoras with which he may have been acquainted. Or it could be that Theodore was actually commenting on both those anaphoras: modern western liturgists, until recently used to only a single canon or prayer of consecration, are too prone to overlook the difficulty of the preacher whose tradition used more than one anaphora. It could be, therefore, that Theodore never composed an anaphora, and that the Catechetical Lectures represent an attempt to comment on a tradition which knew both a version of Byzantine Basil, and the anaphora to which the name of John Chrysostom was later attached.

Whatever the truth of the anaphora or anaphoras reflected in the Catechetical Lectures, it is the intention of this study to show that Botte's estimation of Theodore is preferable to that of Wagner's, though it will be argued that Mar Abbas, or whoever composed Theodore, needed only a knowledge of the Catechetical Lectures, and not any separate traces of the anaphora underlying it.

In his paper on Theodore, Webb made the suggestion that the anaphora may have resulted from a need to shorten Nestorius, though he gave no reference for this view. He was almost certainly referring to Bayard H. Jones, who in a series of papers argued that Addai and Mari was a seventh-century abbreviation of Nestorius.[17] He wrote of the Anaphora of Theodore:

> On the other hand, *Theodore*, for all its free, vigorous, and independent treatment, contains practically nothing that is not in *Nestorius*, and cannot be regarded as anything but an abbreviated version of that original.[18]

Jones' view of Addai and Mari is totally flawed, but his estimation of Theodore has much in its favor.

POSSIBLE SOURCES OF THE ANAPHORA OF THEODORE

Addai and Mari

The majority of liturgists are satisfied that Addai and Mari is a very early anaphora, and that it pre-dates Theodore.[19] Any similarities in theme and language between the two anaphoras would suggest that the compiler of Theodore was consciously dependent upon the much older and established East Syrian anaphora. The similarities can be tabled as follows:[20]

Theodore	Addai and Mari
confess your Holy Name . . . . . . O God the Father . . . your only-begotten Son our Lord Jesus Christ and the Holy Spirit, for ever and ever . . . who through your only-begotten Son the Word . . . created and established the heaven and the earth and all that is therein;	Worthy of praise . . . is the adorable and glorious Name of the Father and of the Son and of the Holy Spirit, who created the world by his grace.

For before you . . . stand a
thousand thousand and myriad
myriads of holy angels; these
. . . hallow your great and
Holy Name in constant praise.
And you have, O Lord, in your
grace, made even the feeble
race of mortal man worthy to
lift up glory and honor, with
all the companies of those on
high . . .
(*post-Sanctus*)
. . . before your great and
awful Name we kneel and adore;
and with us all the companies of
those above praise and give
thanks, for your unspeakable
grace.

For us men and for our
salvation, . . . God the Word
. . . when he descended from heaven
and put on our
humanity, a mortal body . . .
who was delivered for our
sins, and rose that we might
be justified.

(*after the institution narrative*)
And as we have been commanded, so
we your lowly, weak and
miserable servants have
gathered together, that by
permission of your grace we
may perform this great and
dread and holy and divine
mystery . . .

Now also, O Lord, lo this oblation is
offered, before your great and dread
Name, for all the holy Catholic
Church, that you may cause your
peace and tranquility to dwell in the
midst of her all the days of the world.

Your majesty, O Lord, a thousand thousand heavenly beings
worship and myriad myriads of
angels . . . glorify your Name.
(*post-Sanctus*)
And with these heavenly powers
we give thanks to you, O Lord,
even we, your lowly, weak and
miserable servants, because
you have effected in us a
great grace which cannot be
repaid.

in that you put on our
humanity . . .
And you forgave us our debts.
You justified our sinfulness . . .

(*after intercessory material*)
And we also your lowly, weak
and miserable servants, who are
gathered together and stand
before you at this time have
received by tradition of the
example which is from you
rejoicing . . . performing this
great and dread mystery . . .[21]
. . . in the commemoration of the
body and blood of your Christ
which we offer to you upon the
pure and holy altar as you have
taught us. And grant us your
tranquility and your peace all
the days of the world.

Yea, our Lord and our God, accept
from us in your grace this sacrifice
of praise, which is the reasonable
fruit of our lips, that it may be a
good memorial before you of the
righteous of old time and of the
holy prophets, of the blessed
apostles and of the martyrs and
confessors, of bishops and doc-
tors, of priests and deacons and o
all the children of the holy
Catholic Church . . .

you, O Lord, in your unspeakable
mercies make a gracious remembrance for all the upright and just
fathers . . . the holiness of the
prophets, apostles, martyrs and
confessors, and bishops and
priests and deacons, and of all
the children of the holy Catholic
Church . . .

And may there come upon us and
upon this oblation the grace of the
Holy Spirit; may he dwell and rest
upon this bread and cup . . . may he
bless and hallow and seal them . . .

May he come, O Lord, your
Holy Spirit and rest upon this
oblation of your servants, and
bless and hallow it . . .[22]

And whoso in true faith eats of
this bread and drinks of this cup,
may they be to him, O Lord, for
the pardon of debts and forgiveness of sins, and a great hope of
resurrection from the dead,
and for the salvation of his
body and of his soul and for
life and glory for ever and
ever.

that it may be to us, O Lord,
for

the pardon of debts and the
forgiveness of sins, and a great
hope of resurrection from the
dead and

new life in the Kingdom of
heaven . . .

From this comparison it would seem that a number of parts of
Theodore are simply elaborated and expanded material from the
earlier East Syrian Anaphora of Addai and Mari—Praise of the
Name, the Antiochene/East Syrian introduction to the *Sanctus*,[23] the
ancient Syriac manner of referring to the incarnation, "putting on our
humanity"; the intercessory material of Addai and Mari is incorporated in the intercessions of Theodore, and the epiclesis is simply an
expansion.

Nestorius

The tradition concerning the compilation of this anaphora is that,
like that of Theodore, it was translated from the Greek by Mar Abbas

when he went to Constantinople.[24] It is certainly a translation from Greek, and, as has been shown by Bayard Jones, Botte, Wagner, and myself, it has been largely culled from Byzantine Basil and St. John Chrysostom, with (*pace* Jones) some elements from Addai and Mari.[25] Bayard Jones was correct to note that a great deal of the vocabulary of Theodore is already to be found in Nestorius.

Theodore

Nestorius

(*trinitarian opening*)

(*trinitarian opening*)

(*post-Sanctus*)

God the Word, who is the light of your glory, and the brightness from you and the image of your Being . . .

God the Word, the hidden offspring of your bosom, who, being in your likeness and the brightness shining from you and the image of your Being . . . (See Basil post-*Sanctus*)

and by the Holy Spirit, the Spirit of Truth, who is from you the Father, all rational natures visible and invisible, are strengthened and sanctified and made worthy to lift up praise . . .

knowledge of the Holy Spirit, the Spirit of Truth, who proceeds from you, O Father, and is of the hidden essence of your Godhead, in whom all rational natures visible and invisible are strengthened and sanctified and perfected and fulfilled. (See Basil)

For before you, O God the Father of Truth, and before your only-begotten Son our Lord Jesus Christ, and before the Holy Spirit, stand a thousand thousand and myriad myriads of holy angels . . .

For before your Trinity, O Lord, stand a thousand thousand and myriad myriads of angels and archangels . . . (see Chrysostom)

Verily, O Lord, you are holy and glorious for ever and ever. Holy are you, O God the Father of Truth, holy also is your only-begotten Son our Lord Jesus Christ, holy in truth also is the Holy Spirit, Divine Essence uncreated, Maker of all things . . .

Holy are you indeed and glorious are you in Truth . . .
Holy also is your only-begotten Son our Lord Jesus Christ, with the Holy Spirit, who is eternally with you . . . (See Basil)

. . . the only-begotten God the
Word, who is the likeness of God,
counted it not robbery to be the
equal of God, but emptied
Himself and took the likeness
of a servant, when He descended
from heaven and put on our
humanity, a mortal body and a
reasonable, intelligent and
immortal soul, of the holy
virgin by the power of the
Holy Spirit;

God the Word . . . who being in
your likeness . . . thought it not
robbery to be your equal (See
Basil), but he emptied Himself and
took the likeness of a servant,
perfect man . . .

of a reasonable, intelligent and
immortal soul . . . even a passible
nature formed by the power of the
Holy Spirit;

(*intercessions*)

And for all our fathers, the
bishops and periodeutae and
priests and deacons who are in
this ministry of truth, that
they may stand and minister
before you purely and worthily
and holily . . .
and for your sinful and
offending servant . . .

And for all our fathers the
bishops . . . and for all priests who
fulfill their office before you . . . and
for all deacons who hold the mysterie
of the faith in pure conscience . . .

And for your frail servant whom
you have by your grace
made worthy to offer before you
this oblation.

And for the fruits of the earth and
the temperature of the air, that the
crown of the year may be blessed
by your grace.

For the fruits of the earth and
the temperature of the air that
the crown of the year may be
blessed by your grace.

It has already been suggested that the epiclesis of Theodore is an
expansion of Addai and Mari, though like Nestorius, Theodore
petitions for the *grace* of the Holy Spirit to come.

THE CATECHETICAL HOMILIES OF
THEODORE OF MOPSUESTIA

It is my contention that the compiler of Theodore also knew the
Catechetical Lectures, and this influenced him at particular points in
his composition of Theodore, particularly in the order and selection
of material.

Thus an explicit trinitarian opening is suggested by the Catechetical Lectures:

> The right praises of God consist in professing that all praises and all glorifications are due to Him, inasmuch as adoration and service are due to Him from all of us . . . he says "the greatness of the Father." He adds also "and of the Son," because the same thing that is due to the Father is also due to the Son, who is really and truly a Son with identical substance . . . He adds necessarily in the same sentence: "and of the Holy Spirit", and confesses that the Spirit is also of Divine substance.[26]

The form of the *Sanctus* in Theodore has, as has been noted above, parallels in Addai and Mari and in Nestorius. However, the explicit *trinitarian setting* of the *Sanctus* in Theodore, and the explicit mention of *humanity joining with the choirs of heaven* could have been encouraged by the Catechetical Lectures:

> He asserts that praises and glorifications are offered at all times, and before all other (beings), to this eternal and Divine nature, by all the visible creatures and by the invisible hosts . . . The doctrine of the Trinity was also revealed at that time when one Godhead was proclaimed in three persons . . .

> It is necessary, therefore, that the priest should, after having mentioned in this service the Father, the Son, and the Holy Spirit, say: "Praise and adoration are offered by all the creatures to Divine nature" . . . We ought to think of them (seraphim) and to offer a thanksgiving that is equal to theirs. Indeed, the Economy of our Lord granted to us to become immortal and incorruptible, and to serve God with the invisible hosts . . .[27]

And reflecting on the vision of Isaiah,

> . . . we all stand in reverential fear while we bow our heads, as if unable even to look at the greatness of this service. And we make use of the words of the invisible hosts, in order to make manifest the greatness of the grace which has been so unexpectedly outpoured upon us.[28]

The trinitarian post-*Sanctus*, and the use of Philippians 2:6-7 also finds confirmation in the Catechetical Lectures:

> . . . the priest proceeds with the holy service and says before anything else: "Holy is the Father, holy also is the Son, and holy also the Holy Spirit" in order to proclaim that they are the eternal and holy nature . . . He afterwards makes mention also of the

> ineffable grace of (God) for which He made manifest the Economy
> which took place in Christ, and by which the One who was in the
> form of God was pleased to take upon Him the form of a servant,
> so that He might assume a perfect and complete man for the
> salvation of all the human race.[29]

Finally, it may also have been the Catechetical Lectures which influenced one particular point in the epiclesis of Theodore. In both Addai and Mari and Nestorius the request is made for the Spirit, or the grace of the Spirit, to come upon the oblation. In the Catechetical Lectures Theodore of Mopsuestia speaks of an epiclesis where the activity of the Spirit is concerned for the elements *and* the communicants.[30] The Anaphora of Theodore prays:

> And may there come *upon us* and upon this oblation the grace of
> the Holy Spirit.

If the above comparisons are valid, then they strongly suggest that Theodore is an anaphoral *pasticcio*, put together mainly with material from Addai and Mari, and Nestorius, and some ideas from the Catechetical Lectures. However, it does not follow that Theodore should be regarded as an anaphora of secondary importance; on the contrary, there are certain elements of the Anaphora of Theodore which point to it being a careful blending of traditional Syrian concepts, classic Antiochene Christology, and Theodore of Mopsuestia's eucharistic drama.

THE THEOLOGY OF THE ANAPHORA OF THEODORE

The Christology of Theodore was condemned by the Council of Constantinople (553) as being Nestorian, and he was branded as the father of the Nestorian heresy. Prior to this condemnation, however, apart from "Alexandrian" circles, Theodore was regarded as having been a respected orthodox theologian. Indeed, Theodore's Christology was simply a well-developed version of the hitherto classic "Antiochene" approach to the person of Christ, which took seriously the manhood of Christ. East Syria espoused the cause of Nestorius, but in the early years of schism, it was expedient to appeal to the teachings of Theodore. The Anaphora of Theodore seems to reflect both the ancient Syriac view of the incarnation and the Christological concerns of Theodore.

Robert Murray has drawn attention to the fact that "Christ put on the body," the image of clothing, is the Syrian Fathers' favorite way of describing the incarnation.[31] It occurs in the Acts of Judas Thomas and the Didascalia, and Aphrahat who draws on the Diatessaron rendering of John 1:14, "the Word became body (*pagrâ*) and dwelt in us."[32] Ephraem often speaks of Christ's body as a garment he put on:

> The Firstborn was clothed in the body;
> it was the veil of his glory.
> The immortal Bridegroom
> will shine forth in this robe.[33]

This particular approach to Christology is in harmony with the "Antiochene" approach which was developed by Theodore, with a concern for the *homo assumptus*, indwelling and clothing. For Theodore, so Sullivan argued, the *homo assumptus* was not apparently simply human nature, but the particular man Jesus, who could be distinguished from the Word.[34] Sullivan observed:

> Thus he speaks of "Our Lord and Saviour Jesus Christ". Jesus is the name of "the one assumed", of "the one born of Mary". Jesus is "this man assumed for our salvation". For our sakes God "clothed himself with our Lord Jesus, a man, and by the resurrection from the dead made him pass to a new life and made him sit at his right hand."[35]

For Theodore—as for "Antiochene" Christology in general—the free obedience of the manhood, and its co-operation with the *Verbum assumens* was extremely important, and hence his concern with Philippians 2:7ff.[36] At the same time Theodore was renowned among his contemporaries for his strong repudiation of Apollinarianism.

It becomes apparent that the Anaphora of Theodore preserves the traditional "Antiochene" approach to Christology. The opening praise follows Theodore[37] in distinguishing between the Son who is God the Word, through whom the Father created and established the heaven and the earth and all that is therein; and "your only-begotten Son our Lord Jesus Christ" who is now in heaven. Likewise the Christological section of the post-*Sanctus* makes considerable use of Philippians 2:7ff, and again speaks of God the Word who put on our humanity (preserving the phraseology of Addai and Mari), but, in refuting Apollinarianism, the humanity is defined as "a mortal body and a reasonable, intelligent and immortal soul." The dispensation "which had been prepared in your foreknowledge from before the foundation of the world" also recalls one of Theodore's emphases.[38]

This Christology seems to underlie the phraseology later in the Anaphora of Theodore where the eucharist is described as a mystery (*rāzâ*). Thus before the institution narrative:

> And with His holy apostles in that night in which He was
> betrayed, He celebrated this great and holy and divine mys-
> tery . . .

And immediately afterwards:

> And as we have been commanded, so we your lowly, weak and
> miserable servants have gathered together that by permission of
> your grace we may perform this great and dread and holy and
> divine mystery, wherein was great salvation (wrought) for the
> whole race of man . . .

Later the eucharistic action is described as "the mystery of the
Lamb of God which takes away the sin of the world."

The use of *rāzâ* in earlier Syriac literature denotes, in the singular,
a religious symbol, especially an Old Testament type, and also part
of God's plan which the type signified. In the Anaphora of Theodore
it refers to the action of the eucharist, which is a "type" of the whole
salvific work of Christ, particularly his passion, death, and resurrection. This harmonizes with the dominant thought in the Catechetical
Lectures. As Greer points out, for Theodore

> The Liturgy itself is a symbolic representation, an *anamnesis* of
> the resurrection of our Lord. This is the chief way in which the
> Eucharist is connected in Theodore's mind to our Lord's life,
> death, and resurrection. However, the Eucharist also represents
> our Lord's Passion. The Last Supper, and the words of institu-
> tion recited on that occasion, are taken by Theodore to refer
> specifically to Good Friday. Thus the Eucharist is not so much a
> "memorial" of the Last Supper as of the events of the Passion.[39]

Thus in the Catechetical Lectures Theodore taught:

> In contemplating with our eyes, through faith, the facts that are
> now being re-enacted: that He is again dying, rising and ascend-
> ing into heaven, we shall be led to the vision of the things that had
> taken place beforehand on our behalf.[40]

Elsewhere he wrote of the placing of the elements on the altar:

> We must also think of Christ being at one time led and brought
> to His Passion, and at another time stretched on the altar to be
> sacrificed for us.[41]

This symbolism was not new in the Syrian tradition, as the anonymous commentary published by Rahmani and Brock, and probably
contemporary with Chrysostom, illustrates.[42] However, Theodore

develops the symbolism considerably, concentrating on the death of Christ:

> We must first of all realise that we perform a sacrifice of which we eat. Although we remember the death of our Lord in food and drink, and although we believe these to be the remembrance of his Passion—because he said: "This is my body which is broken for you, and this is my blood which is shed for you"—we nevertheless perform, in their service, a sacrifice; and it is the office of the priest of the New Testament to offer this sacrifice, as it is through it that the New Covenant appears to be maintained. It is indeed evident that it is a sacrifice, but not a new one and one that (the priest) performs as his, but it is a remembrance of that other real sacrifice (of Christ).[43]

Theodore also notes that the sacrifice may be pleaded for the living and the dead:

> The priest performs Divine service in this way, and offers supplication on behalf of all those of whom by regulation mention is to be made always in the Church; and later he begins to make mention of those who have departed, as if to show that this sacrifice keeps us in this world, and grants also after death, to those who have died in the faith, that ineffable hope which all the children of the Sacrifice of Christ earnestly desire and expect.[44]

This intercession is, however, directly related to the obedience and exaltation of Christ:

> He calls "intercession" not a supplication made for us in words, as this intercession is made in deeds, because through His ascension into heaven He makes intercession for us to God and is anxious that all of us should ascend into heaven to Him.[45]

The mystery of the eucharist is a celebration of the "type" of the obedient life, the passion, and heavenly intercession through the sacrifice of the cross. It is significant, therefore, that the Anaphora of Theodore has an "obedience" Christology, the institution narrative defining the passion, and then the mystery of the Lamb of God—the sacrifice of the cross and heavenly intercession—is pleaded in the intercessions.

As already noted, the Anaphora of Theodore—unlike the anaphora presupposed in the Catechetical Lectures—has an epiclesis which follows the intercessions. Elsewhere I have suggested that although this may simply reflect the archaic East Syrian pattern of Addai and

Mari, it might also be a result of a thorough application of the theology of the eucharistic drama as found in the Catechetical Lectures.[46]

In many Syrian anaphoras the terminology of the epiclesis recalls the operation of the Spirit and Power of God at creation and the incarnation. Common vocabulary includes "come," "hover," "overshadow," "dwell," and "rest upon."[47] In the Anaphora of Theodore this common stock of vocabulary is reproduced; the grace of the Spirit is asked to come, dwell, and rest upon the bread and cup, and the eschatological fruits of communion are also listed.

The Catechetical Lectures, however, emphasize another aspect of the epiclesis which completed Theodore's overall drama of the liturgy. For Theodore, one prime role of the Spirit was to give life to the entombed body of Christ. On the Creed he writes:

> He shows by his words (1 Cor. 15:45) that Christ our Lord was changed in His body, at the resurrection from the dead, to immortality by the power of the Holy Spirit.[48]

And he could also write:

> Indeed, even the body of our Lord does not possess immortality and the power of bestowing immortality in its own nature, as this was given to it by the Holy Spirit; and at its resurrection from the dead it received close union with Divine nature and became immortality and instrumental for conferring immortality on others.[49]

Explaining the purpose of the epiclesis, Theodore could say:

> Indeed, the body of our Lord, which is from our nature, was previously mortal by nature, but through the resurrection it moved to an immortal and immutable nature . . . In this same way, after the Holy Spirit has come here also, we believe that the elements of bread and wine have received a kind of anointing from the grace that comes upon them, and we hold them to be henceforth immortal, incorruptible, impassible, and immutable by nature, as the body of the Lord was after the resurrection.[50]

The epiclesis in the Anaphora of Theodore has nothing specific to suggest this type of understanding: the concept is "incarnational," with eschatological benefits for the communicants. However, the *structure* of the Anaphora of Theodore gives perfect expression to Theodore's theological drama. The obedient manhood is stressed; the institution narrative recalls the passion; the passion is pleaded in the intercessions which follow, through the mystery of the Lamb; and the sacrificed body is revivified through the epiclesis, so that the "types" of the sacrificed body and blood become the risen and life-giving body and blood of Christ.

The anaphora presupposed by the Catechetical Lectures does not give a perfect expression of Theodore's drama, since the epiclesis (resurrection) comes *before* the intercessions. There, death and resurrection are pleaded; but in the Anaphora of Theodore it is the passion which is pleaded, as Theodore taught.

Is this overly subtle?[51] Perhaps. However, Narsai recognized the drama implicit in the East Syrian pattern. In Homily 17 he could speak of "The awful King, mystically slain and buried,"[52] and could warn:

> Be not taken up with vain thoughts of earthly things: look upon Him that is now mystically slain upon the altar.[53]

And with regard to the intercession and the epiclesis:

> To this effect the priest prays before God, and he asks of Him that He will graciously accept the sacrifice which he offers unto Him. On behalf of all is the living sacrifice sacrificed in the midst of the Church; and this sacrifice helps and profits all creatures. By that supplication which the priest makes on behalf of all classes all his sins and offences are forgiven him.
>
> . . . The Spirit descends upon the oblation without change (of place) and causes the power of the Godhead to dwell in the bread and wine and completes the mystery of our Lord's resurrection from the dead.[54]

Gabriel Qatraya also commented on this drama; the mysteries are performed in memory of the passion, death, and resurrection of our Lord.[55] However:

> When the priest calls the Spirit and it broods over, he joins the body to the blood and the blood to the body (that) is the mystery of the return of his soul into His body and of His resurrection from the dead. For, the priest mystically vivifies the body by the work of the Spirit.
>
> That after the overshadowing the priest does no more sign over the mysteries because the mystery is perfected by the dissolving. At this hour we remove incense from the sacrifice because the corruption, for which was the embalming, is dissolved.[56]

Of course, both Narsai and Qatraya drew on the teaching of the Catechetical Lectures, and they were also aware of other earlier eucharistic teachings.[57] However, the *structure* of the anaphoras of

Nestorius and Theodore—and particularly that of Theodore—gave excellent structural expression of the theology found in the Catechetical Lectures. In addition, I suggest, the Anaphora of Theodore gives excellent *linguistic expression* to "Antiochene" Christology and the eucharistic drama of the Catechetical Lectures.

Notes

1. B. Botte, "Les anaphores syriennes orientales," in *Eucharisties d'orient et d'occident*, vol. 2 (Paris: Editions du Cerf, 1970) 7-24.

2. G. Wagner, *Der Ursprung der Chrysostomusliturgie*, Liturgie-wissenschaftliche Quellen und Forschungen, vol. 59 (Münster: Aschendorff, 1973) 51-72.

3. D. Webb, "The Anaphora of Theodore the Interpreter"; see also "Le sens de l'anaphore de Nestorius," in *La Liturgie: Son sens, son esprit, sa méthode* [Conférences St-Serge, Paris 1981], Bibliotheca Ephemerides Liturgicae - Subsidia, vol. 27 (Rome: CLV-Edizioni Liturgiche, 1983) 349-372. Mention should also be made of J.M. Sánchez Caro, *Eucaristía e Historia de la Salvación* (Madrid: Biblioteca Autores Cristianos. La Editorial Catolica, 1983) 365-380.

4. Bryan D. Spinks, "Eucharistic Offering in the East Syrian Anaphoras," *Orientalia Christiana Periodica* 50 (1984) 347-371 (reprinted as Chapter 5 in the present volume).

5. Leontius of Byzantium, *Contra Nestorianos et Eutychianos*, PG 86:1368c.

6. F.E. Brightman, "The Anaphora of Theodore," *Journal of Theological Studies* 31 (1930) 160-164.

7. A. Mingana, *Commentary of Theodore of Mopsuestia on the Lord's Prayer and the Sacraments of Baptism and the Eucharist*, Woodbrooke Studies, vol. 6 (Cambridge: Heffers, 1933); also *Commentary of Theodore of Mopsuestia on the Nicene Creed*, Woodbrooke Studies, vol. 5 (Cambridge: Heffers, 1932).

8. Botte, "Les anaphores" 13.

9. This information is given in the headings to the anaphoras of Theodore and Nestorius in a number of manuscripts; see Spinks, "Eucharistic Offering" 355.

10. Botte, "Les anaphores" 18.

11. Wagner, *Der Ursprung* 52.

12. Ibid. 53-54.

13. Ibid. 61.

14. Ibid. 63.

15. E. Mazza, "La struttura dell'Anafora nelle Catechesi di Teodoro di Mopsuestia," *Ephemerides Liturgicae* 102 (1988) 147-183.

16. Ibid. 174.

17. Bayard H. Jones, "The History of the Nestorian Liturgies," *Anglican Theological Review* 46 (1964) 157-176; Jones, "The Formation of the Nestorian Liturgy," *Anglican Theological Review* 48 (1966) 276-306.

18. Jones, "The History" 168-169.

19. Bryan D. Spinks, *Addi and Mari - The Anaphora of the Apostles: A Text for Students*, Grove Liturgical Study, vol. 24 (Bramcote: Grove Books, 1980).

20. The translation of the Anaphora of Theodore is based on the Urmiah translation; that of Addai and Mari is my own (see note 19).

21. In *Addai and Mari - The Anaphora of the Apostles*, I suggested that this was a later addition to the underlying common anaphora, since it is absent from *Sharar*. I am now of the opinion that the Maronite version did in fact remove or abandon this paragraph, and that it did belong to the early version of the anaphora.

22. *Sharar* confirms that "bless and hallow it" has been added to the original text of Addai and Mari, perhaps here borrowed from the Anaphora of Theodore.

23. Bryan D. Spinks, *The Sanctus in the Eucharistic Prayer* (Cambridge: Cambridge University Press, 1991).

24. See note 9. The English text is based on the Urmiah text.

25. Jones, "The History" and "The Formation"; Botte, "Les anaphores"; Wagner, *Der Ursprung*; Spinks, "Eucharistic Offering."

26. Woodbrooke Studies, vol. 6, p. 100.

27. Ibid. 100-101.

28. Ibid. 102.

29. Ibid. 102-103.

30. Ibid.

31. Robert Murray, *Symbols of Church and Kingdom: A Study in Early Syriac Tradition* (Cambridge: Cambridge University Press, 1975) 69ff.

32. Ibid. 71.

33. *Carmina Nisibena* 43, 20-21, cited in Murray, *Symbols* 76.

34. Francis A. Sullivan, *The Christology of Theodore of Mopsuestia*, Analecta Gregoriana, vol. 82 (Rome: Gregorian University Press, 1956) 221.

35. Ibid.

36. Ibid. 232-233. Nestorius was also concerned with Philippians 2:7ff; see J.F. Bethune-Baker, *Nestorius and His Teaching* (Cambridge: Cambridge University Press, 1908) 123ff.

37. R. Greer, *Theodore of Mopsuestia: Exegete and Theologian* (London: Faith Press, 1961) 50-51.

38. Ibid. 51-52.

39. Ibid. 81.

40. Woodbrooke Studies, vol. 6, p. 83.

41. Ibid. 85.

42. I.E. Rahmani, *I fasti della Chiesa Patriarcale Antiochene* (Rome: Tipographia Deela R. Accademia Del Lincei, 1920); S.P. Brock, "An Early Syriac Commentary on the Liturgy," *Journal of Theological Studies*, New Series 37 (1986) 387-403.

43. Woodbrooke Studies, vol. 6, p. 79.

44. Ibid. 105.

45. Ibid. 81.

46. Spinks, "Eucharistic Offering."

47. S.P.Brock, *The Holy Spirit in the Syrian Baptismal Tradition*, The Syrian Churches Series, vol. 9 (Poona: Anita Press, 1979).

48. Woodbrooke Studies, vol. 5, p. 110.

49. Woodbrooke Studies, vol. 6, p. 75.

50. Ibid. 104.

51. See K.W. Stevenson, *Eucharist and Offering* (New York: Pueblo, 1986) 50.

52. R.H. Connolly, *The Liturgical Homilies of Narsai*, Texts and Studies, vol. 8 (Cambridge: Cambridge University Press, 1909) 7.

53. Ibid. 11-12.

54. Ibid. 20; see p. 18 where supplication is made.

55. G. Vavanikunnel, *Homilies and Interpretation on the Holy Qurbana* (Changanacherry: Sandesanilayam Publications, 1977) 88.

56. Ibid. 99.

57. Narsai, according to Vööbus, was influenced by Aphrahat; see A. Vööbus, "Regarding the Theological Anthropology of Theodore of Mopsuestia," *Church History* 33 (1964) 115ff; according to Brock, "An Early Syriac Commentary," he also drew upon the teaching of Chrysostom, and, according to Brock, on the anonymous commentary.

5

Eucharistic Offering
in the East Syrian Anaphoras

WHILE THE CONCEPT OF THE EUCHARIST AS "OFFERING" AND "SACRIFICE" continues to be an area of debate among systematic theologians, in an exploratory article entitled "Anaphoral Offering: Some Observations on Eastern Eucharistic Prayers," Kenneth Stevenson alerted liturgists to the fact that little work had so far been undertaken on this subject, and in a preliminary survey of the material, urged the importance of the task not only for liturgical theology, but also for ecumenism.[1] This present study attempts to further our understanding of the development of anaphoral offering by closely examining the concepts underlying the East Syrian anaphoras—Addai and Mari, Nestorius, and Theodore the Interpreter. The method adopted has been to place each of these anaphoras in some historical context, and then to examine the terminology each uses. The study does not take into account the *kuššāpê* prayers, since these private prayers of the priest do not seem to belong to the earliest strata of the anaphoras. They are not mentioned by Narsai in his commentary in the fifth century, nor by Pseudo-George of Arbel in the ninth century, and they are absent from the *Mar Eša'ya* manuscript, which is our earliest manuscript of the anaphoras.[2] This does not mean that the *kuššāpê* are post-tenth century and of no significance. However, they reflect a theology of the *ordained priesthood vis à vis* the eucharist, which is surely a subsequent development from the general underlying theology of an anaphora, which is of the *church vis à vis* the eucharist.

ADDAI AND MARI

Although the "original form"[3] or "common tradition"[4] of Addai and Mari continues to be the object of discussion, and various reconstructions have been offered, the text which has come down to us in the manuscript tradition remains reasonably fixed. The *Mar Eša'ya* text published by W.F. Macomber and dated by him as tenth/ eleventh century, is usually regarded as a fairly reliable text in most instances,[5] and may now be evaluated by reference to the parallel text in Maronite *Sharar*.[6] While the problem of whether or not the anaphora underwent abbreviation in the time of Iso'yabh III continues to remain unsolved, there is little in the text of the anaphora which could not be given a third- or even a second-century dating.[8] While some scholars have preferred to see a tripartite structure to the anaphora based upon the *ghānātā and qānōne* (surely these rubrical directions are to some degree artificial?), I have preferred to follow a bipartite structure, marked by the two doxologies.[9] The anaphora has five references to offering—one in the opening dialogue, one in the doxology marking the first part of the anaphora, and three references in the second part.

1.   The oblation (*qurbānā*) is offered (*metqarab*) to God the Lord of all.

The first reference occurs in the opening dialogue and is said by the priest. Unfortunately the authenticity—and therefore the precise significance—of this statement is uncertain. Robert J. Ledogar has suggested that since "Let us give thanks to the Lord" introduces the anaphora in all traditions except the Nestorian, "The oblation is offered to God the Lord of all" may be a later modification, and a similar view is suggested by A. Gelston.[10] W.F. Macomber subjected this entire section of the anaphora to a critical comparison with the dialogues of the Blessing of Baptismal Oil, Maronite *Sharar*, the Blessing of Water in James of Sarug, and that found in the Catechetical Lectures of Theodore of Mopsuestia, and concludes that it may originally have been the final phrase of a longer declaration of the meaning and intentions of the eucharistic prayer, which in the Nestorian tradition replaced "Let us give thanks to the Lord."[11] The reconstruction of the "original" form which he offers is not entirely convincing. In complete contrast, Louis Bouyer suggests that "here we are touching upon a very ancient testimonial of the sacrificial sense given to the "eucharist" from the time when it was still simply expressed in the terminology of the Synagogue prayers."[12] Thus, it is difficult to know whether we have here a very early reference to the eucharist as an oblation, or simply a later doctrinal statement which now heads this ancient anaphora.

In defense of it being an early reference, one may point to the Didache, where in chapter 14 the eucharist is referred to as a sacrifice (θυσία) with references to Malachi 1:11 and Matthew 5:23, without necessarily meaning the elements of bread and wine.[13] It is also interesting that in the Old Syriac Gospels, Matthew 5:23-24, Προσφέρω is translated by qrb, and δῶρον by qurbānā, and in the second century it may well have been given a eucharistic interpretation.[14] Again, in the Syrian Odes of Solomon, 20:1-5 we find the following:

> I am a priest of the Lord,
> And Him I serve as a priest.
> And to Him I offer the offering (mqareb na qurbānā) of His
>   thought,
> For His thought is not like the world, nor like the flesh,
> Nor like them who worship according to the flesh.
> The Offering of the Lord (qurbāneh d'marya) is righteousness
> And purity of heart and lips.
> Offer (qareb) thy inward being faultlessly
> And let not thy compassion oppress compassion;
> And let not thyself oppress anyone.[15]

Oblation here is clearly spiritual and ethical, and not the eucharist. However, in view of the usage of the Old Syriac Gospels, and the belief that the offering of Christ was the perfect offering (Heb 10:5-10)—of which the eucharist was a proclamation—the adoption of the qrb / qurbānā terminology for the eucharist could well have occured at an early date. It is also important to observe that in the anaphora in the Apostolic Tradition, and in the Strasbourg Papyrus Greek 254 which some recent studies have suggested is a *complete* anaphora,[16] the prayer itself regards the eucharist as an offering. The fact, therefore, that this terminology occurs in the dialogue, while unique to the East Syrian family, does not necessarily mean that it is a later innovation. Its precise meaning is another matter, and it is doubtful that we can be precise. Clearly it refers to what is happening and what is about to happen; the bread and wine have been placed on the holy table, and a prayer is about to be recited. The content of the prayer itself must to a certain extent determine the understanding of this statement in the dialogue.

2.   The second reference to offering occurs in the first doxology which concludes: "And for all your aids and graces towards us let us offer (*naseq*) to you glory, and honor, and thanksgiving and worship, now and at all times," though these words are not actually given in the *Mar Eša'ya* text, which simply gives the introduction, "And for all."[17] The verb *slq*, raise up, or offer, is used in the *Peshitta* version of Hebrews 11:17, offering up (Προσέφερεν) of Isaac, and Hebrews 13:20 to render ὁ ἀνγαγὼν. In Addai and Mari it is used to sum up the focus of the first part of the anaphora—an offering up of praise and thanks to the Name, revealed as Father, Son, and Holy Spirit (see Mal 1:11; Mt 28:17; Odes of Solomon 6:7, 19:2, 23:22) who created and redeemed mankind. Worship is offered by the angelic beings, and with them men also give thanks because of redemption through the incarnation.[18] Thus far the only *qurbānā* is one of praise offered (*naseq*) over bread and wine for what the elements call the mind—the salvific work of God.

3.   In the *ghāntā* commemorating the upright and just fathers, these "fathers" are described as those "who have been pleasing before you in the commemoration (*'uhdānā*) of the body and blood of your Christ which we offer (*mqarbīnan*) you upon this pure and holy altar as you have taught us." God is asked to remember the just fathers who have in the past been gathered around the altar. The thought here, following on from the first part of the anaphora, seems to be to associate the righteous dead with the praises of the angelic beings and with the living, and, as A. Gelston notes, is brought into only the loosest connection with the sacrifice either of the eucharist or the cross.[19] What is offered (*qrb*) upon this pure and holy altar (suggested by Matthew 5:23-24?), is the "commemoration of the body and blood of your Christ." The root *'hd*, commemorate, according to Ledogar, carries with it the understanding of proclamation;[20] the bread and wine would thus be understood as a proclamation of the body and blood of Christ—a visual and mysterious proclamation of redemption (showing forth the Lord's death). This is perhaps expounded further in the paragraph which follows. The originality and identity of this paragraph, which has no parallel in *Sharar*, has been much disputed, but it nevertheless explains the rite as "rejoicing and glorifying and magnifying and commemorating and praising and performing this great and dread mystery of the passion and death and resurrection of our Lord Jesus Christ." What is offered, therefore, is the performing of a rite which is a mystery, but which is done so in a context of offering up praise.

4.   In the epiclesis God is asked that the Holy Spirit may come and rest upon this "oblation" (*qurbānā*). Botte has argued convincingly—and Maronite *Sharar* seems to give confirmation—that the petition "bless and hallow it" is an interpolation from Nestorius and Theodore.[21] The early form seems to have asked for the Holy Spirit to rest on the oblation so that fruits of communion may be secured. In this context *qurbānā* refers to the elements of bread and wine.

5.   The final doxology again offers up (*masqînan*) thanksgiving and worship. The thought here seems to be that through the blood of Christ, the redeemed can see God face to face, and offer worship.

In summary, Addai and Mari sees the eucharist as an oblation (*qurbānā*). There may well be some correlation here between *qurbānā* and δυρον (Mt 5:23-24; Mk 7:1; see δυρα in the anaphoras of St. Basil and St. John Chrysostom.[22]) The *qurbānā* consists of praise and thanksgiving for redemption. Redemption has been gained by the death of Christ, who left us an example for the church to perform. This example is the mystery of redemption, and is a commemoration (proclamation) of the body and blood of Christ, which witnesses not only to the sacrifice of the cross, but is also a mystery of the passion and resurrection. The Holy Spirit rests on this oblation so that redemption gained by Christ may be imparted through this commemoration. The whole action—praise and commemoration—is offered by the church to the Name. The reference to giving thanks with open mouths and uncovered faces (see Ps 51:15; 2 Cor 3:18, Rv 22:3-4) indicates that the offering is in close association with the worship of heaven—of the angelic beings, and the eternal priesthood of Christ. Where offering verbs are used, *qrb* is used for the commemoration of the body and blood of Christ, whereas *slq* is used for verbal praise. This may indicate—though it is impossible to be precise—that the reference in the opening dialogue which uses the verb *qrb*, whether early or late, refers to the eucharistic action, i.e., the rite of commemorating with the bread and wine. Yet, just as "Let us give thanks" in other anaphoras includes offering within the anaphora, so in Addai and Mari, "The oblation is offered to God the Lord of all" includes praise and thanksgiving within the anaphora.

THE ORIGIN OF THE ANAPHORAS OF NESTORIUS AND THEODORE

The origin and authorship of these two anaphoras remain to some extent shrouded in mystery. However, since their origin may explain any differences in terminology and theology of eucharistic offering to that of Addai and Mari, we must give some consideration to this prior question.

It is practically certain that, despite their titles, the composition of these Nestorian anaphoras has nothing to do with either Nestorius or Theodore of Mopsuestia. Nestorian they almost certainly are, for although they do not emphasize an obvious Nestorian Christology, they appear to have been compiled after the East Syrian Church had espoused the teachings of the deposed bishop Nestorius, and the writings of his mentor, Theodore of Mopsuestia.

One source of information comes from Leontius of Byzantium. Writing c. 531 A.D. about Theodore, he says:

> He also dared to add another evil, not second to those we have spoken of. He concocted another anaphora besides that which had been handed down to the churches by the Fathers; he had neither respect for that of the apostles, nor for that which was written by the great Basil in the Spirit himself, judging this worthy of esteem. In which anaphora he filled the rite with blasphemies (for they were not prayers).[23]

While it has been pointed out that the context would fit Nestorius rather than Theodore,[24] it does affirm that an anaphora was composed quite deliberately, and that it post-dates the Anaphora of the (Twelve) Apostles (we assume an earlier version of Greek Chrysostom)[25] and that of St. Basil (Byzantine Basil). Leontius knew that the anaphora was attributed by the Nestorians to one of their founding fathers.

A second source of information is provided by the headings to these anaphoras found in some manuscripts, though they are relatively late. The heading of the Anaphora of Nestorius in the Cambridge University Library *Ms ADD 1984 (Alqosh 1707 AD.)* is as follows:

> By the grace of God we begin to write the Hallowing (*quddaša*) of my Lord Nestorius, Patriarch of Byzantium, the martyr, but not unto blood, and persecuted for the truth of Orthodox praises. Mar Abbas the Great, the Catholicos of blessed memory, when he went up to Rome, (Constantinople) translated the Hallowing of Mar Nestorius from Greek into Syriac and established all things, as Mar John the Catholicos indicates in the mimra which he composed on the Fathers.

And the Anaphora of Theodore:

> In the power of our Lord Jesus Christ we begin to write the
> Hallowing of my Lord Theodore, the Interpreter of godly books,
> which Mar Abbas the Catholicos set forth and translated from
> Greek into Syriac when he went up to Rome (Constantinople),
> and he translated it with the help of Mar Thomas the doctor, of
> Edessa.

Similar headings are found in Cambridge University Library Mss,
ADD 2046 A and *ADD 2046 B* (Nestorius only), and British Library *Ms.
ADD. 7181.* If these headings are anything more than worthless
legend—and the internal evidence seems to give them partial vindi-
cation—then they too imply a West Syrian Greek origin for Nestorius
and Theodore. The mention of Mar Abbas the Great and Mar Thomas
of Edessa gives a clue to a possible dating. The former was Catholicos
between the years 540 and 522 A.D., and Mar Thomas of Edessa died
in 533 A.D. A date in the second or third decades of the sixth century
perhaps suggests itself.

However, this picture is complicated by two further factors. In the
first place, regarding dating, Narsai seems to presuppose the existence of an anaphora or anaphoras of the type represented by Nestorius
and Theodore rather than Addai and Mari. While it may be that
Narsai's Homily XVII has been edited, the recent work by Jammo
suggests that it is, nevertheless, mainly the work of Narsai.[26] It has
been alleged that the anaphora underlying Narsai's comments corre-
sponds neither to Nestorius nor to Theodore, but was therefore
another Nestorian anaphora of a related type.[27]

However, there is no necessity for an East Syrian theologian of the
fifth century to quote from anaphoras with the accuracy demanded
by twentieth-century liturgical scholarship; furthermore, if Narsai
was commenting upon the anaphora *in general*, when his Church
used at least three, then it is understandable that his comments do not
correspond exactly to the contents of one particular anaphora. (Western liturgical scholars, until recently used to only a single *canon missae*
or Prayer of Consecration, seem to have overlooked the problem
facing commentators of traditions where several anaphoras were in
regular use.) Indeed, Narsai seems to switch with considerable ease
between parts of Nestorius and parts of Theodore. Thus, "For when
the time of the passion of the Lifegiver of all was arrived, He ate the
legal passover with His disciples"[28] seems to allude to the narrative
of institution in Nestorius, "For when the time came when he should
be betrayed for the life of the world, after He had kept the Passover
with His disciples according to the law of Moses . . .," whereas "He

commends the priests and periodeutae and deacons; and he entreats that they may be in holiness and purity"[29] only has a parallel in Theodore: "And for all our fathers the bishops and periodeutae and priests and deacons who are in this ministry of truth, that they may stand and minister before thee purely and worthily and holily . . ." If therefore, as seems likely to the present writer, Narsai knew Nestorius and Theodore, then it suggests that these anaphoras were in existence in some form in the fifth century.

A final complicating factor is the relationship between Nestorius and Theodore. Nestorius, as has been pointed out by Botte,[30] and the careful analysis of Bayard Jones,[31] is a skillful conflation of both St. Basil and Greek Chrysostom (or Twelve Apostles), and Addai and Mari. Botte writes:

> La comparaison entre l'anaphore de Nestorius et celle de S. Jean Chrysostome nous permet d'y apporter certains correctifs. La parenté entre les deux textes saute aux yeux. Si nous prenons, par exemple, l'action de grâces, Chrysostome se retrouve mot à mot dans Nestorius; mais dans ce dernier il s'y ajoute des développements repris en grande partie à l'anaphore byzantine de S. Basile. D'autre part, Nestorius a gardé des élements propres à la tradition syrienne orientale. Ainsi son épiclèse n'est autre que celle d'Addaï, mais avec l'incise caractéristique; "en les (=le pain et le vin) changeant par ton Saint-Esprit."[32]

G. Wagner also acknowledges the dependence of Nestorius on Chrysostom, though he suggests an early sixth-century date at Constantinople.[33] The question of Theodore is far less certain. Wagner believes that it is an East Syrian adaptation of the anaphora upon which Theodore of Mopsuestia comments in his Catechetical Lectures.[34] Yet at the same time Theodore seems dependent upon Addai and Mari. It may be that Theodore is in fact a compilation based not on an Anaphora of Theodore, but upon his catechetical homilies, with material from Addai and Mari, and possibly even Nestorius; it may well owe its existence to the fact that Nestorius was too lengthy.[35] In considering the terminology and theology of eucharistic offering in these two anaphoras, we shall bear in mind the following probable (Nestorius) and possible (Theodore) derivations:

Addai and Mari St. Basil Twelve Apostles/Earlier Greek Chrysostom	} Nestorius
Catechetical Lectures of Theodore Addai and Mari (Nestorius?)	} Theodore

OFFERING IN NESTORIUS

1.   The dialogue expands the reference to oblation found in Addai and Mari, but this statement is complicated by the fact that the *Mar Eša'ya* text has a less expanded formula than that of the rest of the manuscript tradition, represented by the Urmiah edition. The *Mar Eša'ya* text has:

> The living and reasonable oblation of our first-fruits, and the unslain sacrifice of the Son of our race, our kinsman, for all created things to their utmost bound, is offered to God the Lord of all.[36]

Apart from the words "our kinsman," and with the addition of "the unslain *and acceptable* sacrifice," this is the same formula as that found in the other manuscripts for Theodore. The Urmiah version of this formula in Nestorius is:

> The living and reasonable oblation of our first-fruits, and the unslain and acceptable sacrifice of the Son of our race, which the prophets figured in a mystery, and the apostles proclaimed openly, and the martyrs bought with the blood of their necks, and the doctors expounded in the churches, and the priests sacrificed upon the holy altar, and the holy Levites bare upon their arms, and the nations partook of for the pardon of their debts, and for all created things to their utmost bound is offered to God, the Lord of all.

This would seem to indicate that the opening formulas have undergone later expansion, or it could indicate a certain fluidity regarding the opening formulas of Nestorius and Theodore.[37] It is significant that, if these anaphoras were compiled from West Syrian sources, the authors did not take over the dialogue of the Greek sources. May this not suggest that the basic formula, "The oblation is offered to God the Lord of all," was so firmly embedded in East Syrian tradition that the compilers dared not replace it, but chose to expand it? Nevertheless, the expansion is an interesting and considerable theological qualification of the short formula in Addai and Mari. The *qurbānā* is "living and reasonable" (Rom 12:1), of our first-fruits (Jesus - 1 Cor 15:20, 23), and also the "unslain (and acceptable) sacrifice (*debhā la' dabai'a'* [*waqebla'*]) offered (*metqarab*) to God. However, this formula seems to be a theological summary of the prayer and action.

2. In the first *ghāntā* we have three sacrificial references, all apparently concerned with verbal praise though with ritual overtones.

(a) Do thou, my Lord, give us utterance in opening our mouths, that we may offer (*nqareb*) to thee with a contrite heart and humble spirit, the spiritual fruit of our lips, even a reasonable service.

Here Ephesians 6:19 has been woven together with words from St. Basil:

καὶ σοὶ προσφέρειν ἐν καρδία συντετριμμένη καὶ πνεύματι ταπεινώσεως τὴν λογικὴν ταύτην λατρείαν ἡμῶν.

(b) Now to Thee and to Thy only begotten Son and to the Holy Spirit we offer (*masqîn*) continual praise without ceasing, because all things are Thy work.

While this echoes the doxology of Addai and Mari, it also echoes St. Basil. Bayard Jones points out that the reading of the manuscripts, "Thy work" may be rendered "Thy servants" with only a change in pointing.[38]

παρ' οὗ πᾶσα κτίσις λογικῇ τε καὶ νοερὰ δυναμουμένη σοὶ λατρεύει καὶ σοὶ τὴν ἀΐδιον ἀναπέμπει δοξολογία ὅτι τὰ σύμπαντα δοῦλα σά

(c) and we give Thee thanks for this service (*tešmeštā*) and we beseech thee to accept (*tqablîh*) it at our hands.

This seems to have been borrowed from Chrysostom:

εὐχαριστοῦμέν σοι καὶ ὑπὲρ τῆς λειτουργίας ταύτης ἣν ἐκ τῶν χειρῶν ἡμῶν δέξασθαι.

Λειτουργίας may refer to verbal praise, but it more probably refers to the performance of the eucharist itself.

3. (a) The second *ghāntā*, following the *Sanctus*, gives praise for the work of Christ, and leads into the institution narrative with the statement that "he left us the commemoration (*'uhdānā*) of our salvation, this mystery (*'rāzā*) which we offer (*mqarbînan*) before Thee." This is very close to Addai and Mari—the commemoration of the body and blood of Christ which is offered upon the pure and holy altar, and later termed a mystery. However, once again the phraseology seems to have been influenced by St. Basil:

κατέλιπεν δέ ἡμῖν ὑπομνήματα τοῦ σωτηρίου αὐτοῦ πάθους ταῦτα ἃ προτεθείκαμεν κατὰ τὰς αὐτοῦ ἐντολάς.

Of interest here, however, is that while Basil offers (Προτεθείκαμεν) in the past tense, presumably referring back to the placing of the

bread and wine on the altar,[39] Nestorius, using participle and pronoun, expresses a present tense, suggesting that offering is taking
place in the action in the anaphora. Furthermore, the offering seems
to be connected with the recital of the words of institution. The
institution is described as Christ's own passover (surely a sacrificial
connotation), which "we keep for His commemoration as He com-
mitted it unto us until He be revealed from heaven." It is, therefore,
this commemoration, which is a mystery, which is being offered.

(b) The *ghāntā* concludes with further offering (*naseq*) of praise,
honor, confession, and adoration.

4. In the *ghāntā* after the institution we find three references to
offering.

> (a) We offer (*mqarbīnan*) unto thee this sacrifice (*debhā*) living and
> holy and acceptable and glorified and awful and exalted and
> spotless for all creatures and for the holy apostolic catholic
> church . . .

This combination of terminology, some of which is gleamed from
Romans 12:1 and Hebrews 9:14, 12:28, does not have an exact parallel
in our present texts of St. Basil or St. John Chrysostom. Chrysostom,
prior to the epicelsis, reads:

> Ετι προσφέρομέν σοι τὴν λογικήν ταύτην καὶ αναίμακτον
> λατρείαν

which is repeated before the intercessions. Syriac Twelve Apostles
reads at the intercessions:

> Therefore we offer (*mqarbīnan*) to thee, Lord almighty, this
> rational sacrifice (*debhtā*) for all men, for your catholic church. . .

Bayard Jones suggested that St. James was a source here—
Προσφέρομέν σοι, τὴν φοβερὰν ταύτην καὶ αναίμακτον θυσίαν,
in the anamnesis,[40] but it is more likely that the compiler followed
basic ideas found in West Syrian sources without recourse to St.
James, and has developed it in his own way, with a number of
adjectives which is a characteristic of his style. However, it is note-
worthy that now the term sacrifice (*debhā*) rather than simply *qurbānā*
has been introduced into the anaphora itself.

> (b) And for thy frail servant whom thou hast by thy grace made
> worthy to offer (*lamqarābu*) before this oblation (*qurbānā*).

St. Basil seems to have been an inspiration:

> Μνήσθητι Κύριε κατὰ τὸ πλῆθος τῶν οἰκτιρμῶν σου καὶ τῆς
> ἐμῆς ἀναξιότητος· συγχώρησόν μοι πᾶν πλημμέλημα ἑκούσιον

τε καὶ ἀκούσιον καὶ μὴ διὰ τὰς ἐμὰς ἁμαρτίας κωλύσῃς τὴν
χάριν τοῦ ἁγίου σου πνεύματος ἀπὸ τῶν προκειμένων δώρων.

(c) The *ghāntā* concludes with offering (*naseq*) of praise and confession.

5. The final *ghāntā* continues the intercessions, and contains two further references to offering.

(a) We beseech thee, my Lord, and we make supplication before thee; that thou wilt remember over this oblation (*qurbānā*) the fathers and patriarchs, prophets and apostles . . .

This is reminiscent of Addai and Mari, but also of Chrysostom:

῎Ετι προσφέρομέν σοι τὴν λογικὴν ταύτην λατρείαν ὑπὲρ τῶν
ἐν πίστει ἀναπαυσαμένων πατέρων πατριαρχῶν προφητῶν
ἀποστόλων.

(b) The epiclesis:

And may the grace of the Holy Spirit come, O my Lord, and may He dwell and rest upon this oblation (*qurbānā*) which we offer (*mqarbînan*) before thee. May He bless and consecrate it and make this bread and this cup to be the Body and Blood of our Lord Jesus Christ . . .

Botte[41] points out that Nestorius follows the form of Addai and Mari, but the compiler has also expanded it from St. Basil:

καὶ προθέντες τὰ ἀντίτυπα τοῦ ἁγίου σώματος καὶ αἵματος τοῦ
Χριστοῦ σου σοῦ δεόμεθα καὶ σὲ παρακαλοῦμεν ἅγιε ἁγίων
εὐδοκίᾳ τῆς σῆς ἀγαθότητος ἐλθεῖν τὸ Πνεῦμά σου τὸ πανάγιον
εφ᾽ ἡμᾶς καὶ ἐπὶ τὰ προκείμενα δῶρα ταῦτα καὶ εὐλογῆσαι
αὐτὰ καὶ ἁγιάσαι καὶ ἀναδεῖξαι. Τὸν μὲν ἄρτον.

It would appear, therefore, that while Nestorius may be a skillful conflation of St. Basil and a version of St. John Chrysostom (Twelve Apostles), the offering terminology is mainly derived from the former. Much of the theology of offering is simply an amalgam of those ideas found in the Greek West Syrian sources. Thus, in the terminology of St. Basil, there is offering of verbal praise and thanksgiving, described in terms of Hebrews 13:14 and Romans 12:1, which is offered up in praise to the Trinity, and includes thanksgiving for the whole liturgical service (Chrysostom). Following Basil, the commemoration of our salvation is offered. It is at this point that the anaphora develops a different theology from that of the Greek sources. The West Syrian sources have the following sequence: anamnesis, epiclesis, and intercessions. According to Kenneth Stevenson, in Chrysostom the offering is "firmly in the anamnesis, linking the offering with prayer, in epiklesis and intercession."[42] In Basil offering is also found in the anamnesis, epiclesis, and intercessions, though in the latter offering is in the past tense, and seems to refer back to the offertory.[43] Nestorius, however, retains the sequence of Addai and Mari—intercession, epiclesis, doxology, and in so doing, has changed the emphasis. The offering of the eucharistic elements appears to be closely linked with the recital of the institution narrative; there is no anamnesis of the West Syrian type. The offering, which is in the present tense, is made as the words of institution are introduced (described as a commemoration of salvation), and, after their recital, but before the epiclesis, the elements are described as a sacrifice (*debhā*), and it is offered for all creatures and the church. The sacrifice is not connected with the epiclesis. The Spirit is asked to come on the oblation in order to make the elements the body and blood of Christ *after* the intercessions. Thus in Nestorius we have the following general pattern:

Offering of praise (*nqareb, masqîn*)

Offering of the commemoration of our salvation (*mqarbînan*) which is performed by the recitation of that salvation as recorded in the institution.

Pleading the sacrifice (*debha*) (death of Christ) which is commemorated.

Petition for the Spirit to make the oblation life-giving to those who receive it.

OFFERING IN THEODORE THE INTERPRETER

1. The dialogue seems to belong to a "floating" tradition; the *Mar Eša'ya* text simply has the same as Addai and Mari, while the Urmiah edition, as noted above, gives a version similar to the *Mar Eša'ya* formula for Nestorius. Perhaps this suggests that Theodore was indeed compiled to give a shorter anaphora than Nestorius, and no new dialogue was composed for it. However, whatever may be the ultimate origin and relationship of these versions of the dialogue, Theodore, like Nestorius, contains the words *qurbānā, debhā,* and *metqarab.*

2. (a) The first and second *ghānātā* after the dialogue, between which occurs the *Sanctus*, are concerned with an offering of praise. While Addai and Mari and Nestorius imply that the *Sanctus* is offered as praise with the angelic beings, Theodore explicitly makes it so:

> And Thou hast, my Lord, in Thy grace, made even the feeble race of mortal man worthy to offer (*nasqun*) glory and honor, with all the companies of those on high, to thy Almighty sovereignty, even with those who at all times before the majesty of Thy holiness raise their voice to glorify Thy glorious Trinity which in three Persons co-equal and undivided is confessed ... (*Sanctus*) ... we offer (*masqînan*) praise and honor and confession and adoration, to the Father and to the Son and to the Holy Spirit . . . before Thy great and awful Name we kneel and adore, and with us all the companies of those above praise and give thanks for Thy unspeakable grace.

While F.E. Brightman and G. Wagner have suggested that the Anaphora of Theodore could be the work of Theodore of Mopsuestia,[44] this explicit linking of the earthly praise of the church with the celestial worship may well have been suggested to a compiler by the Catechetical Lectures of Theodore:

> The right praises of God consist in professing that all praises and all glorifications are due to Him, inasmuch as adoration and service are due to Him from all of us . . . He asserts that praises and glorifications are offered at all times, and before all other (beings), to this eternal and divine nature, by all the visible creatures and by the invisible hosts . . . He makes mention also of the seraphim, as they are found in the Divine Book singing praise which all of us who are present sing loudly in the Divine song which we recite, along with the invisible hosts, in order to serve God. We ought to think of them and to offer a thanksgiving that is equal to theirs.[45]

This specific praise of the angels seems to take the place of the reference to "offering of the fruit of lips" in Nestorius, and is more akin to the sense of Addai and Mari.

(b) In the second *ghāntā*, as part of the recital of salvation in Christ, Hebrews 9:14 and Colossians 1:18, 20 are joined together.

> who through the eternal Spirit offered (*qareb*) himself without spot to God, and hath sanctified us by the offering (*qurbānā*) of His body once, and made peace by the blood of His cross.

(c) The words of institution carefully articulate the link between the offering of the body of Christ once, and the eucharist as an offering. The Last Supper is described thus:

... he performed this great and holy and divine mystery, taking the bread ...

And as we have been commanded, so we thy weak and frail and miserable servants have come together, that by permission of thy grace we may perform this great and awful and holy and divine mystery, wherein was great salvation (wrought) for the whole race of man.

At the conclusion of this *ghāntā*, praise, thanksgiving, honor, and adoration are offered (*masqînan*).

3. The third *ghāntā*, following the narrative of institution, introduces intercession linked with offering:

(a) Adoration is given for being made worthy to administer (*lamšamašu*) before God this awful and divine service (*tešmešā*) for the salvation of our lives.

b) we offer (*mqarbînan*) before thy glorious Trinity, with a contrite heart and humble spirit this living and holy and acceptable sacrifice (*debhtā*), the mystery of the Lamb of God which taketh away the sin of the world.

(c) that in Thy pitifulness this pure and holy oblation (*qurbānā*) may be accepted in which thou wast well pleased and reconciled regarding the sins of the world.

Here the offering is carefully linked with the performing of the mystery, and the performing is carefully defined as a service for our salvation—the sacrifice, or mystery of the Lamb which taketh away the sin of the world. A careful link is made between the cross, the Last Supper, and the continued performing of the rite.

(d) In the same *ghāntā*, this identity or link having been established, the oblation (*qurbānā*) is offered (*metqarab*) (this occurs twice) for a series of motives in intercession.

(e) The whole rite can be described as a sacrifice of praise (*debhā dᵉtawdita*) which is the reasonable fruit of lips (see Heb 13:15) which is "as a good memorial before Thee of the righteous of old time."

4. In the epiclesis the Spirit is asked to come upon the oblation (*qurbānā*); the epiclesis of Theodore is nearer to the form in Addai and Mari than Nestorius, and omits the words "which we offer" found in the latter.

The theology of offering in Theodore is far more clearly and logically expressed than in Nestorius. First, there is an offering of praise which is explicitly united with the angelic offering of the *Sanctus*. The one offering of Christ was performed as a mystery at the

Last Supper; the church continues to perform the same mystery, and that mystery is a service, a sacrifice and an oblation which is then firmly linked with intercessions. The whole can be described as a sacrifice of praise, the reasonable fruit of lips, suggesting that the service, or mystery, is a proclamation of the sacrifice of Christ. Finally, as in Nestorius, the Holy Spirit is invoked upon the oblation so that it might be life-giving to those who receive it.

THE EAST SYRIAN THEOLOGIES OF OFFERING

From this survey of anaphoral offering in these three East Syrian eucharistic prayers, several interesting and significant observations can be made.

First, regarding terminology (see table), generally the East Syrian anaphoras reserve the verb 'aseq (Aph'el of slq) for offering in connection with praise, and qareb (Pa'el of qrb) for offering in connection with the eucharistic action. An exception to this is found in Nestorius, where nqareb is used for the spiritual sacrifice of the fruit of lips. However, the compiler appears to have been drawing on St. Basil, where the verb is Προσφέρω. It should be noted, however, that the reference in St. Basil does have ritual overtones. The noun used in the East Syrian anaphoras is qurbānā. Judging from the Old Syriac Gospels, qurbānā may be regarded as an equivalent to δῶρον, and is therefore akin to δῶρα found in St. Basil and St. John Chrysostom. In Nestorius and Theodore the term debhā (feminine debhtā in Theodore), sacrifice, is introduced, though apart from the opening dialogue, only after the recital of the institution narrative. This terminology and its context allows other observations to be made.

It would seem legitimate to draw a distinction between Addai and Mari on the one hand, Nestorius and Theodore on the other. The occurrence of qurbānā . . . metqarab in the dialogue of Addai and Mari would seem to be not so much an offertory prayer[46] as a statement of how the eucharistic action was understood. There is no necessity to conclude that it replaced an earlier "Let us give thanks to the Lord," for all anaphoras which contain the latter still regard the eucharist as an offering. In Addai and Mari it seems to refer to the whole eucharistic action—placing the bread and wine on the altar, the recitation of the eucharistic prayer, which is making the commemoration of the body and blood of Christ, and culminating in communion. Indeed, in addition to praise, what Addai and Mari actually offers in the text which has come down to us is "the commemoration of the body and blood of Christ." Kenneth Stevenson seems to be correct when he sees the oblation as unitive, without sequence or development;[47] oblation in this anaphora is left undeveloped.

However, the same conclusion cannot be made for Nestorius and Theodore. Whatever may be the meaning of the dialogue reference in Addai and Mari, in Nestorius and Theodore it seems best understood as a doctrinal summary of the anaphora. In the anaphoras themselves, we would suggest that a clear sequence of development is to be found. In Nestorius this is clouded slightly by the fact that so much of the offering terminology has been lifted from Greek West Syrian anaphoras. Nevertheless, there is a sequence: the offering of praise; the offering of the mystery, which is associated with the recital of the institution narrative; and then pleading this mystery of the passion and death in the intercessions. Only after the intercessions—the pleading of the sacrifice of Christ—is the Spirit invoked to make the oblation life-giving to those who are to receive it. This sequence is even more logically expressed in Theodore. Praise is offered, and this clearly includes the *Sanctus*. The one offering of Christ is celebrated by performing the rite, and there is a clear link between the one sacrifice of Christ, the mystery of the Last Supper, and the performing of that mystery in the church's eucharist. It can be described as a sacrifice and oblation, and is pleaded in the intercessions. Again, only after the death is pleaded is the Spirit invoked to make the oblation life-giving to the communicants.

The sequence of thought in Nestorius and Theodore entails the structure of the anaphora being that which is distinctly East Syrian: institution narrative, (anamnesis) intercessions, epiclesis. The question which poses itself from this is: If Nestorius and Theodore were compiled after West Syrian models (this applies more to Nestorius than Theodore), why was the West Syrian pattern (institution narrative, anamnesis, epiclesis, intercessions) abandoned?

One answer may be that since in Addai and Mari the epiclesis was at the end of the prayer, this was so established in East Syria that the compilers of the Nestorian anaphoras dared not break such a tradition. Yet, clearly, the Maronite community shared no such fetish about the position of the epiclesis, happily using its version of Addai and Mari, *Sharar*, alongside many anaphoras of the West Syrian pattern. The Egyptian Church also used West Syrian anaphoras alongside its own. One wonders whether in fact, in view of the sequence of ideas of offering in Nestorius and Theodore, the change of anaphoral pattern was deliberate, and was connected with the concept of eucharistic offering. Could it be that behind these two Nestorian anaphoras and their structure is a theology suggested by the Catechetical Lectures of Theodore of Mopsuestia?

Theodore describes the eucharist as performing symbolically the remembrance of the death of Christ.[48] Indeed, when the deacons carried out the bread and wine, so Theodore explains, they place it on the altar for a complete representation of the passion.[49] Theodore seems to dwell on this representation of the passion and death—a remembrance of the sacrifice.

> Indeed, He (our Lord) gave us the bread and the cup because it is with food and drink that we maintain ourselves in this world, and He called the bread "body" and the cup "blood", because, as it was His Passion that affected His body which it tormented and from which it caused blood to flow, He wished to reveal, by means of these two objects through which His Passion was accomplished, and also in the symbol of food and drink, the immortal life, in which we expect to participate when we perform this Sacrament from which we believe to derive a strong hope for the future benefits.[50]

And again:

> We must first of all realise that we perform a sacrifice of which we eat. Although we remember the death of our Lord in food and drink, and although we believe these to be the remembrance of his Passion—because He said: "This is my body which is broken for you, and this is my blood which is shed for you"—we nevertheless perform, in their service, a sacrifice; and it is the office of the priest of the New Testament to offer this sacrifice, as it is through it that the New Covenant appears to be maintained. It is indeed evident that it is a sacrifice, but not a new one and one that (the priest) performs as his, but it is a remembrance of that other real sacrifice (of Christ).[51]

Theodore also notes that the sacrifice may be pleaded for the living and the dead:

> The priest performs Divine service in this way, and offers supplication on behalf of all those of whom by regulation mention is to be made always in the Church; and later he begins to make mention of those who have departed, as if to show that this sacrifice keeps us in this world, and grants also after death, to those who have died in the faith, that ineffable hope which all the children of the Sacrament of Christ earnestly desire and expect.[52]

However, Theodore has a particular Christological concern regarding the explanation of the epiclesis. Commenting on the function of the Spirit, Theodore states:

> Indeed, even the body of our Lord does not possess immortality and the power of bestowing immortality in its own nature, as this was given to it by the Holy Spirit; and at its resurrection from the dead it received close union with Divine nature and became immortal and instrumental for conferring immortality on others.[53]

This Christology Theodore applies directly to the epiclesis. Thus, describing the eucharist as representing the passion, he explains:

> It is, therefore, with justice that the same thing is done here with the body which lies on the altar, and which is holy, awe-inspiring and remote from all corruption; a body which will very shortly rise to an immortal nature.[54]

And, explaining the epiclesis:

> Indeed, the body of our Lord, which is from our own nature, was previously mortal by nature, but through the resurrection it moved to an immortal and immutable nature . . . In this same way, after the Holy Spirit has come here also, we believe that the elements of bread and wine have received a kind of anointing from the grace that comes upon them, and we hold them to be henceforth immortal, incorruptible, impassible, and immutable by nature, as the body of our Lord was after the resurrection.[55]

Theodore was, of course, commenting upon a rite which was of the West Syrian type, with the following structure: narrative, anamnesis, epiclesis, intercessions. However, when such a theology of the epiclesis is applied strictly, it might appear (as Cyril of Jerusalem suggests[56]) that the life-giving body of Christ is being offered and pleaded in the intercessions, and not the commemoration of the passion and death. Perhaps it is not too fanciful to suggest that someone with a particular interest in the theology of Theodore—as presumably the compilers of the two Nestorian anaphoras had—might find it more logical to express Theodore's ideas by pleading the passion in the intercessions after the institution narrative, and by leaving the "resurrecting" of the body until the end of the prayer. The life-giving body was not needed for intercession, but for communion to impart immortality. Whatever the merits of this suggestion, Nestorius and Theodore do have a particular theology of offering which is formulated differently from the West Syrian anaphoras, and they deserve more attention from liturgists than they have hitherto received.

H.A.J. Wegman has drawn attention to the possible ecumenical significance of Addai and Mari.[57] While there is a danger that far too much may be claimed for this ancient and enigmatic anaphora, it may be that its undeveloped offering terminology may prove suggestive in ecumenical debate. The eucharist is conceived as an offering up of praise in which the divine economy is recounted. Included in this offering is the commemoration of the body and blood of Christ, for the bread and wine are themselves, "as you have taught us," a proclamation of the divine economy. Because the terminology is left undeveloped, the God-ward and human-ward elements are insepa-rably intertwined. The more developed and articulated concepts found in Nestorius and Theodore the Interpreter provide some insight into how the terminology was developed in one tradition. While these concepts will almost certainly be unacceptable to some theological traditions,[58] the manner in which the two Nestorian anaphoras articulate the connection between the sacrifice of the cross, the Last Supper, the Lord's Supper, and intercession for the church, may prove not entirely unhelpful.

Notes

1. K.W. Stevenson, "Anaphoral Offering: Some Observations on Eastern Eucharistic Prayers," *Ephemerides Liturgicae* 94 (1980) 209-228.

2. W.F. Macomber, "The Oldest Known Text of the Anaphora of the Apostles Addai and Mari," *Orientalia Christiana Periodica* 32 (1966) 335-371, 345-347.

3. J.M. Sánchez Caro, "La anáfora de Addai y Mari y la anáfora maronita Sarrar: intento de reconstrucción de la fuente primitiva común," *Orientalia Christiana Periodica* 43 (1977) 41-69; H.A.J. Wegman, "Pleidooi voor een Tekst van de Anaphora van de Apostelen Addai en Mari," *Bijdragen* 40 (1979) 15-43; Bryan D. Spinks, "The Original Form of the Anaphora of the Apostles: A Suggestion in the Light of Maronite Sharar," *Ephemerides Liturgicae* 91 (1977) 146-161; reprinted as Chapter 2 of this volume.

4. Bryan D. Spinks, *Addai and Mari—The Anaphora of the Apostles: A Text for Students,* Grove Liturgical Study, vol. 24 (Bramcote: Grove Books, 1980); W.F. Macomber, "The Ancient Form of the Anaphora of the Apostles," in *East of Byzantium: Syria and Armenia in the Formative Period* (Washington, D.C.: Dumbarton Oaks Center for Byzantine Studies, 1982) 73-88.

5. Macomber, "The Oldest Known Text."

6. *Anaphorae Syriacae,* vol. 2, fasc. 3 (Rome: Pontificium Institutum Orientalium Studiorum, 1982).

7. S. Hermiz Hammo, "Gabriel Qatraya et son commentaire sur le liturgie chaldéenne," *Orientalia Christiana Periodica* 32 (1966) 39-52; Edward J. Kilmartin, "John Chrysostom's Influence on Gabriel Qatraya's Theology of Eucharistic Consecration," *Theological Studies* 42 (1981) 444-457; Bryan D. Spinks, "Addai and Mari and the Institution Narrative: The Tantalising Evidence of Gabriel Qatraya," *Ephemerides Liturgicae* 98 (1984) 60-67; reprinted as Chapter 3 of this volume.

8. J. Vellian, "The Anaphoral Structure of Addai and Mari Compared to the Berakoth Preceding the Shema in the Synagogue Morning Service, *Le Muséon* 85 (1972) 201-223; Bryan D. Spinks, "The Original Form of the Anaphora."

9. Spinks, "The Original Form of the Anaphora."

10. Robert J. Ledogar, *Acknowledgment: Praise Verbs in the Early Greek Anaphoras* (Rome: Herder, 1968) 27; A. Gelston, "Sacrifice in the Early East Syrian Eucharistic Tradition," in *Sacrifice and Redemption*, ed. S.W. Sykes (Cambridge: Cambridge University Press, 1991) 118-125. I am grateful to Rev. A. Gelston for allowing me to see his script, which was being completed quite independently of my own.

11. W.F. Macomber, "The Maronite and Chaldean Versions of the Anaphora of the Apostles," *Orientalia Christiana Periodica* 37 (1971) 55-84, esp. pp. 58-65.

12. L. Bouyer, *Eucharist*, tr. C.U. Quinn (Notre Dame: University of Notre Dame Press, 1968) 305.

13. A wide variety of explanations have been offered (!) as to its meaning, often with dogmatic presupposition. W. Rordorf and A. Tuilier, *La Doctrine des douze apôtres*, Sources chrétiennes, vol. 248 (Paris: Editions du Cerf, 1978), regard the chapter as the work of a redactor. On the other hand, Joan Hazelden Walker argued that the Didache could be pre-Marcan, and even pre-Pauline, and can see nothing un-Jewish in chapter 14: "Reflections on a New Edition of the Didache," *Vigiliae Christianae* 35 (1981) 35-42, and "A Pre-Marcan Dating for the Didache: Further Thoughts of a Liturgist," *Studia Biblica* 1978 (Sheffield: Sheffield University Press, 1980) 403-411.

14. New Testament commentators tend to regard the text as referring to temple offering. E. Schweizer, *The Good News According to Matthew* (London: SPCK, 1975) notes that verses 23-26 are in the second person singular, and perhaps were added later (p. 115). In a document written after the destruction of the temple, one wonders whether there is already here an overt reference to the eucharist.

15. J.H. Charlesworth, *The Odes of Solomon* (Missoula, MT: Scholars Press, 1977) 84-85.

16. E. Kilmartin, "Sacrificium Laudis: Content and Function of Early Eucharistic Prayers," *Theological Studies* 35 (1974) 268-287; W.H. Bates, "Thanksgiving and Intercession in the Liturgy of St. Mark," in *The Sacrifice of Praise*, ed. Bryan D. Spinks (Rome: CLV-Edizioni Liturgiche, 1981) 107-

119; H.A.J. Wegman, "Une anaphore incomplète?" in *Studies in Gnosticism and Hellenistic Religions*, ed. R. Van Den Broek and M.J. Vermaseren (Leiden: E.J. Brill, 1981) 432-450; G.J. Cuming, "The Anaphora of St. Mark: A Study in Development," *Le Muséon* 95 (1982) 115-129 (read as a master theme at the Oxford Patristic Conference, 1979). See Bryan D. Spinks, "A Complete Anaphora? A Note on Strasbourg Gr. 254," *Heythrop Journal* 25 (1984) 51-55.

17. Clearly the *Mar Eša'ya* text is an abbreviation, presupposing the doxology. This should caution against a simple acceptance of the *Mar Eša'ya* readings.

18. See 1 Corinthians 4:9. C.K. Barrett, noticing that only "world" has a definite article, translates "to the whole world, angels and men alike," and comments on Paul's thought: "*Angels and men* between them constitute the world's population." See *The First Epistle to the Corinthians* (London: A. & C. Black, 1968) 110. *Pace* E.C. Ratcliff, I have consistently argued that the *Sanctus* is original in Addai and Mari and not an intrusion. This view is now shared by W.F. Macomber, in "The Ancient Form of the Anaphora" and T.J. Talley, "The Eucharistic Prayer: Tradition and Development," in *Liturgy Reshaped*, ed. Kenneth Stevenson (London: SPCK, 1982) 48-64.

19. Gelston, "Sacrifice in the Early East Syrian Eucharistic Tradition."

20. Ledogar, *Acknowledgment: Praise Verbs* 35.

21. B. Botte, "L'épiclèse dans les liturgies syriennes orientales," *Sacris Erudiri* 6 (1954) 48-72.

22. For a discussion on the similarities between Addai and Mari, see W.E. Pitt, "The Origin of the Anaphora of the Liturgy of St. Basil," *Journal of Ecclesiastical History* 12 (1961) 1-13.

23. Leontius of Byzantium, *Contra Nestorianos et Eutychianos*, PG 86:1368c.

24. G. Khouri-Sarkis, "L'origine syrienne de l'anaphore byzantine de saint Jean Chrysostome, *L'Orient syrien* 7 (1962) 3-68, esp. p. 7, note 8.

25. Ibid.

26. S. Hermiz Jammo, *La Structure de la messe chaldéenne du début jusqu'à l'anaphore: Etude historique*, Orientalia Christiana Analecta, vol. 207 (Rome: Pontificium Institutum Orientalium Studiorum, 1979) 13-25.

27. E.C. Ratcliff, "A Note on the Anaphoras Described in the Liturgical Homilies of Narsai," in *Biblical and Patristic Studies in Memory of Robert Pierce Casey*, ed. J.N. Birdsall and R.W. Thomson (Freiburg and New York: Herder, 1963) 235-249.

28. R.H. Connolly, *The Liturgical Homilies of Narsai*, Texts and Studies, vol. 8 (Cambridge: Cambridge University Press, 1909) 16.

29. Ibid. 18.

30. B. Botte, "Les anaphores syriennes orientales," in *Eucharisties d'orient et d'occident*, vol. 2 (Paris: Editions du Cerf, 1970) 7-24.

31. Bayard H. Jones, "The Formation of the Nestorian Liturgy," *Anglican Theological Review* 48 (1966) 276-306.

32. B. Botte, "Les anaphores syrienne" 11.

33. G. Wagner, *Der Ursprung der Chrysostomusliturgie*, Liturgiewissenschaftliche Quellen und Forschungen, vol. 59 (Münster: Aschendorff, 1973) 63-72.

34. Ibid. 51-63.

35. Bayard H. Jones, "The History of the Nestorian Liturgies," *Anglican Theological Review* 46 (1964) 157-176.

36. I am grateful to Dr. W.F. Macomber for kindly supplying me with transcripts of the *Mar Eša'ya* texts of Nestorius and Theodore.

37. There is also the possibility that the *Mar Eša'ya* manuscript has abbreviated the text.

38. Jones, "The Formation of the Nestorian Liturgy" [note 31 above] 285.

39. So Stevenson, "Anaphoral Offering" 212.

40. Jones, "The Formation of the Nestorian Liturgy" [note 31 above] 294.

41. Botte, "Les anaphores syriennes orientales" 11.

42. Stevenson, "Anaphoral Offering" 212.

43. Ibid.

44. F.E. Brightman, "The Anaphora of Theodore," *Journal of Theological Studies* 31 (1930) 160-164; G. Wagner, *Der Ursprung*.

45. A. Mingana, *Commentary of Theodore of Mopsuestia on the Lord's Prayer and on the Sacraments of Baptism and the Eucharist*, Woodbrooke Studies, vol. 6 (Cambridge: Cambridge University Press, 1933) 100-101.

46. See Stevenson, "Anaphoral Offering" 221, though he too questions the suggestion.

47. Ibid. 227.

48. Mingana, 74, 99, 103.

49. Ibid. 86.

50. Ibid. 74-75.

51. Ibid. 79, see p. 80.

52. Ibid. 105.

53. Ibid. 75.

54. Ibid. 86-87.

55. Ibid. 104.

56. *Catecheses Mystagogicae* 5, 8.

57. Wegman, "Pleidooi voor een Tekst" 15-43.

58. Although not including intercessions for the church and the world, the eucharistic prayers of the Church of Scotland's *Book of Common Order* 1940 and 1979 have much in common with the concepts of Nestorius and Theodore. See J.M. Barkley, "'Pleading His Eternal Sacrifice' in the Reformed Liturgy," in *The Sacrifice of Praise*, ed. Spinks, 123-140.

TABLE OF OFFERING TERMINOLOGY IN THE EAST SYRIAN ANAPHORAS

	ADDAI AND MARI	NESTORIUS	THEODORE
Dialogue	qurbānā...metqarab	qurbānā...debhā ...metqarab	qurbānā...debhā ...metqarab
Ghāntā 1		nqareb masqîn tešmešā. . tqablîh	nasqun
Sanctus (Qānonā)			
Ghāntā 2		'rāzā...mqarbînan (institution narrative)	masqînan qareb...qurbānā (institution narrative)
Doxology (Qānonā)	naseq	naseq	masqînan
Ghāntā 3	'uhdānā...mqarbînan	mqarbînan...debhā lamqarābu...qurbānā	lamšamašu...tešmešā mqarbînan...debhtā qurbānā...netqabal metqarab qurbānā metqarab qurbānā debhā dᵉtawdita qurbānā (epiclesis)
Doxology (Qānonā)	qurbānā (epiclesis)	naseq	_____
Ghāntā 4	masqînan	qurbānā qurbānā...mqarbînan (epiclesis)	
Doxology (Qānonā)	_____	_____	

6

The Epiclesis in the East Syrian Anaphoras

THE PURPOSE OF THIS STUDY IS TO EXAMINE THE EPICLESIS AS FOUND IN THE THREE East Syrian anaphoras, Addai and Mari, Nestorius, and Theodore. This study is based on a number of presuppositions which I have attempted to establish in previous studies on this anaphoral tradition.

1. My first presupposition is that Addai and Mari is the earliest of the three anaphoras and, since it shares much in common with the Maronite anaphora called *Sharar*, points to at least a fourth-century date, but possibly as early as the second or third centuries.

2. The second presupposition is that a comparison between Addai and Mari and *Sharar* enables us to establish what is most likely to have been the earliest text of the common form of the underlying anaphora.

3. My third presupposition is that Nestorius dates from the late fifth- or early sixth-century and is an East Syrian adaptation of anaphoras similar to those of St. John Chrysostom/Twelve Apostles, Byzantine Basil, and Greek James.

4. Finally, my last presupposition is that Theodore has been compiled from Addai and Mari, Nestorius, and in a few instances, from the Catechetical Lectures of Theodore of Mopsuestia; the compiler gave expression in the anaphora to the Christology and soteriology of Theodore of Mopsuestia.

In its strict etymological sense, "epiclesis" can refer to any invocation addressed to God. The earliest form of what may be termed a liturgical epiclesis seems to be the transliteration of the Aramaic *Maranatha*, found in 1 Corinthians 16:22, and its Greek translation in Revelation 22:20, ἔρχου, Κύριε Ἰησοῦ. Maranatha is also found in Didache 10:6. The verb is "come," in the imperative, addressed to the Risen Lord.[1] In both 1 Corinthians 16:22 and Revelation 22:20 the formula may be a deliberate echo of eucharistic worship, the Risen Lord being asked to come and manifest his presence.[2] In the Didache it follows a prayer over the bread, though it is far from clear as to the precise nature of the rite which is being described.

There is evidence which suggests that the early consecratory epiclesis, even if not derived directly from this primitive formula, nevertheless has close affinities with it in the use of the verb "come." The apocryphal Acts of Thomas contains a eucharistic epiclesis addressed to Christ, to "come (ἐλθέ) and communicate with us." There follows a long list of epithets of Christ, each prefaced with "come." Of significance too is the variant reading in the Lucan version of the Lord's Prayer, Luke 11:2: your Holy Spirit come (ελθάτω) upon us and cleanse us." Here, of course, the petition is in the mouth of Christ to the Father, and its authenticity is extremely doubtful. It might be possible, however, to see in this the epiclesis finding its way into the Lord's Prayer, since it is followed by the petition "give us this day our daily bread." Certainly the Acts of Thomas establish "come" as a verb used in early Syrian sources. Among Syro-Byzantine anaphoras, St. Basil uses the verb "come," but otherwise the usual verb is "send." Addai and Mari uses the verb "come," as does Maronite *Sharar*. The other two East Syrian anaphoras also preserve the term "come," even though some of their apparent sources used the verb "send." There is every reason, then, to regard the East Syrian epiclesis as preserving a link with the earliest forms of the eucharistic epiclesis.

Addai and Mari and Sharar

The texts of the epiclesis of Addai and Mari and *Sharar* are as follows:[3]

Addai and Mari	Sharar
May he come, O Lord, your Holy Spirit and rest upon this oblation of your servants, and bless and	And may he come, O Lord your living and Holy Spirit, and dwell and rest upon this obla-

hallow it, that it may be to us, O Lord, for the pardon of debts and the forgiveness of sins, and a great hope of resurrection from the dead and a new life in the kingdom of heaven with all who have been pleasing before you.

tion of your servants. And may it be to those who partake for the pardon of debts and the forgiveness of sins and for a blessed resurrection from the dead and a new life in the kingdom of heaven for ever.

In his recent study of Addai and Mari, Anthony Gelston has argued that the anaphora was addressed to the Father, and he is not persuaded that *Sharar*'s address to the Son is the earlier.[4] I am still inclined to side with Macomber on this point, and regard the address to the Son as being the earlier form.[5] The epiclesis would therefore have been addressed to Christ (see Galatians 4:6, 1 Corinthians 15:45, which have suggested "living" as a qualification of the Holy Spirit, and Hebrews 9:14).

Some manuscripts of Addai and Mari have "living" and "dwell," so it is not immediately apparent as to whether these are a later expansion or not. "Rest" and "dwell," in that order, are found in Nestorius; in *Sharar* they are reversed, and reflect the *Peshitta* version of Isaiah 11:2. If the majority of the manuscripts of Addai and Mari are followed, "rest" would seem to be the earlier term used, and "dwell" is a later expansion.

On the other hand, the words "bless and hallow" are not in the Maronite prayer. Here Bernard Botte has made out a good case for seeing these two verbs as being interpolated from the epiclesis of Nestorius.[6] As far as other differences between Addai and Mari and *Sharar* are concerned, Gelston is surely correct in suggesting that *Sharar*'s "*and* may it be" rather than "*that* it may be" is due to a textual corruption with *waw* being confused for *dalet*.[7] Gelston prefers Addai and Mari's "to us" rather than *Sharar*'s "those who partake," and rejects both "great hope" and "blessed" which qualify "resurrection," and he also discounts the readings of both anaphoras after "kingdom of heaven." This would give an earlier form of epiclesis as follows:

> And may he come, O Lord, your Holy Spirit, and rest upon this oblation of your servants, that it may be to us for the pardon of debts and the forgiveness of sins, and for the resurrection from the dead, and for new life in the kingdom of heaven.

However, Theodore's epiclesis does actually give some support for both Addai and Mari's and *Sharar*'s additions after "kingdom of heaven." Theodore has "the new life in the kingdom of heaven *and glory* for ever," and later mentions "those who have been well pleasing to your will." Could it be that both were accepted forms at some stage in its early history?

In this epiclesis the request is for the Holy Spirit to rest upon the oblation, but subsequent requests are for the eschatological fruits of communion. This epiclesis may be compared with that of the anaphora of the Apostolic Tradition attributed to Hippolytus, and dated c. 215 A.D., though that epiclesis uses the term "send." Here Addai and Mari seems to have preserved a very early form of the eucharistic epiclesis, and the main function of the Spirit is to give the communicants the eschatological gifts.

Nestorius

The epiclesis in Nestorius is as follows:

> And may there come, O Lord, the grace of your Holy Spirit and rest and dwell upon this oblation which we offer before you. And may he bless and hallow and make this bread and this cup the body and blood of our Lord Jesus Christ, and change and hallow them by the working of your Holy Spirit so that the taking of these glorious and holy mysteries may be to all who receive them for eternal life and resurrection from the dead and pardon of the body and soul and into the light of knowledge and uncovered face towards you and to eternal salvation which you have promised through our Lord Jesus Christ, that he may hold together in one accord the bond of love and peace and that we may be one body and one spirit as we are called in one hope of calling.[8]

In a study published in 1908 Baumstark drew attention to the apparent dependence of the Anaphora of Nestorius upon that of the Greek Anaphora of St. John Chrysostom,[9] and this has been supported and extended in subsequent studies by Bayard Jones and Bernard Botte.[10] It would certainly seem that the compiler knew of Greek anaphoras similar to Byzantine Basil and St. James; and he either knew St. John Chrysostom's anaphora, or some form from which this and the Anaphora of the Twelve Apostles have evolved. If the epiclesis of Nestorius is compared with that of Addai and Mari and the Syro-Byzantine anaphoras, it will be seen that the epiclesis of Nestorius is a compilation from these sources.

1. Nestorius has retained the initial petition of Addai and Mari, though requesting "the grace" of the Holy Spirit, and the anaphora is unquestionably addressed to the Father. It has also qualified "oblation" with "which we offer before you."

2. "Bless and hallow and make" would seem to have been derived from Byzantine Basil ("bless and hallow") and St. James or Chrysostom ("make"). "Change," *metabalon*, is also found in Chrysostom.

3. The eschatological fruits of communion have been expanded from Addai and Mari, and the compiler has drawn on Scripture—2 Corinthians 3:18, 2 Corinthians 4:6, Acts 15:25, Philippians 2:2, and Ephesians 4:4-6. However, these have been suggested by his probable sources. Twelve Apostles has "health of soul and body" and "enlightenment of mind" and makes reference to the "life-giving mysteries." Unity is the theme of Byzantine Basil, and St. James has "eternal life" and "sanctification of souls and bodies."

Theodore

The epiclesis of Theodore has the following:

> And may there come the grace of the Holy Spirit upon us and upon this oblation and rest and reside (*thagen*) upon this bread and upon this cup. And may he bless and hallow and seal them in the Name of the Father and of the Son and of the Holy Spirit. And by the Power of your Name may this bread become the holy body of our Lord Jesus Christ, and this cup the precious blood of our Lord Jesus Christ. And whosoever in true faith eats from this bread and drinks from the cup, may they be for them, O Lord, for the pardon of debts, the remission of sins, a great hope of the resurrection from the dead, and salvation of body and soul, the new life in the kingdom of heaven and glory for ever. And make us worthy by the grace of our Lord Jesus Christ that with all those who have been well pleasing to your will and have been led according to your commandments we may rejoice in the kingdom of heaven, in the good things that will be prepared and will not pass away.[11]

As with Nestorius, we find here that the earlier East Syrian terminology found in Addai and Mari has been retained, though as in Nestorius, it is "the grace" of the Holy Spirit which is requested from the Father. The immediate inference is that the compiler of Theodore has taken it from Nestorius. However, both may have been inspired by the Catechetical Lectures of Theodore of Mopsuestia, whose work was extremely important for East Syrian theologians. Theodore, referring to the invocation over the baptismal waters, mentions that it is the grace of the Holy Spirit which is requested to come upon the water.[12] As regards the eucharist, Theodore wrote:

> It is with great justice, therefore, that the priest offers ... prayer and supplication to God that the Holy Spirit may descend, and that grace may come therefrom upon the bread and wine that are laid ... the priest prays that the grace of the Holy Spirit may come also on all those present ... .[13]

There are, in fact, two things in the opening sentence of the epiclesis in this East Syrian anaphora which seem to reflect the lectures of Theodore:

1. The use of "the grace" of the Holy Spirit.
2. Unlike Addai and Mari and Nestorius, but like Theodore's lecture (but also Byzantine Basil, St. James, and St. John Chrysostom), the epiclesis prays for the grace of the Holy Spirit to come upon the communicants as well as the oblation.

Theodore has retained the verb *nesre/tesre* ("rest") used in Addai and Mari and Nestorius, but has also used the verb *gn* which means hovering, or overshadowing, or residing. The verb is used in Syriac James (Greek James has *epiphoitesan*), but in the *Peshitta* is used for the activity of the Spirit at Luke 1:35. As we have seen, the terms "bless and hallow" are found in Nestorius and are found in several Syro-Byzantine anaphoras. "Seal" is peculiar to Theodore, though it also occurs in the East Syrian baptismal Ordo. The invocation of the "Power of your Name" recalls Acts of Thomas 27, "Come, Power of grace," though there the name is that of Christ rather than the blessed Trinity. The "holy" body and "precious" blood are found in St. James.

The eschatological fruits of communion are the compiler's own rearrangement of those found in Addai and Mari. He has added the "salvation of body and soul," perhaps a variant on Nestorius' "pardon of body and soul." The plea for worthiness (a separate plea in Nestorius) finds a parallel in Twelve Apostles, and Chrysostom prays for the "fullness of the kingdom." The compiler has, however, retained the eschatological fruits of Addai and Mari, reproducing them all.

* * * * * *

In his study of the versions of St. Basil and the relationship of Basil to St. James, John Fenwick has set out two methods of fourth-century anaphoral construction techniques:[14]

1. The versions of St. Basil show how one method was by expansion and rewriting within the anaphora.

2. St. James seems to have been the result of conflation of the type of anaphora known to Cyril (or John) of Jerusalem with that of St. Basil.

It would be hazardous to make final conclusions about the East Syrian anaphoras of Nestorius and Theodore simply on the basis of the epiclesis. What the epiclesis in this tradition would seem to witness to is a combination of methods (1) and (2). Addai and Mari and the early East Syrian traditions are not abandoned, but are supplemented by conflating material from Basil, Chrysostom/Twelve Apostles, and St. James. At the same time the material has been adapted and modified to form something which is new and distinct. The epicleses of these East Syrian anaphoras point then to yet a further technique of anaphoral construction.

Notes

1. "Marana tha, Our Lord comes." It would be possible to translate this as "Maran atha, Our Lord has come," but the former is generally thought to make better sense.

2. J.A.T. Robinson, "The Earliest Christian Liturgical Sequence," *Journal of Theological Studies*, New Series 4 (1958) 38-41; G.B. Caird, *The Revelation of St. John the Divine* (London: Black, 1966).

3. My translation of the *Mar Eša'ya* text of Addai and Mari, and the critical text of *Sharar* by J.M. Sauget, *Anaphorae Syriacae*, vol. 2, fasc. 3 (Rome: Pontificium Institutum Orientalium Studiorum, 1973).

4. A. Gelston, *The Eucharistic Prayer of Addai and Mari* (Oxford: Clarendon Press, 1992).

5. Bryan D. Spinks, "The Original Form of the Anaphora of the Apostles: A Suggestion in the Light of Maronite Sharar," *Ephemerides Liturgicae* 91 (1977) 146-161; reprinted as Chapter 2 of the present volume; W.F. Macomber, "The Ancient Form of the Anaphora of the Apostles," in *East of Byzantium: Syria and Armenia in the Formative Period*, ed. N.G. Garsoian, T.F. Mathews, and R.W. Thomson (Washington, D.C.: Dumbarton Oaks Center for Byzantine Studies, 1982) 73-88.

6. B. Botte, "L'épiclèse dans les liturgies syriennes orientales," *Sacris Erudiri* 6 (1954) 48-72.

7. Gelston, *The Eucharistic Prayer* 109.

8. I have used the Urmiah text here.

9. A. Baumstark, "Die Chrysostomosliturgie und die syrische Liturgie des Nestorios," in *Chrysostomika* (Rome, 1908) 771-857.

10. Bayard H. Jones, "The History of the Nestorian Liturgies," *Anglican Theological Review* 46 (1964) 157-176; Jones, "The Formation of the Nestorian

Liturgy," *Anglican Theological Review* 48 (1966) 276-306; B. Botte, "Les anaphores syriennes orientales," in *Eucharisties d'orient et d'occident*, vol. 2 (Paris: Editions du Cerf, 1970) 7-24.

11. I have used the critical text of Jacob Vadakkel, *The East Syrian Anaphora of Mar Theodore of Mopsuestia* (Kottayam: Oriental Institute of Religious Studies India, 1989).

12. A. Mingana, *Commentary of Theodore of Mopsuestia on the Lord's Prayer and the Sacraments of Baptism and the Eucharist* (Cambridge: W. Heffer, 1933) 55.

13. Ibid. 104.

14. John Fenwick, *Fourth Century Anaphoral Construction Techniques*, Grove Liturgical Study, vol. 45 (Bramcote: Grove Books, 1986).

7

Priesthood and Offering in the *Kuššāpê*, of the East Syrian Anaphoras

IT IS THE PURPOSE OF THIS CHAPTER TO EXAMINE SOME OF THE *KUŠŠĀPÊ* PRAYERS which are found in the East Syrian anaphoras. The root meaning of *kššp* is "to speak softly or whisper," and in the *Ethpa'al*, "to pray in a low voice, or supplicate earnestly." The *kuššāpê* prayers may be generally defined as private supplicatory prayers, said by the priest kneeling, and they invariably reflect a sense of unworthiness felt by the priest as he approaches his duties at the eucharist. Not unnaturally, the subject matter of these prayers is priesthood and offering.

It is perhaps hardly surprising that the *kuššāpê* have received little attention from scholars. The reason for this neglect is the general consensus among liturgists that these prayers represent a much later intrusion into the anaphoras, corresponding to Dix's classification of the "Third Stratum" in the completion of the shape of the liturgy.[1] The tendency of modern liturgical scholarship is to regard such tertiary developments as unhealthy, which may be true; but this, coupled with the quest for the primitive, means that such phenomena tend to be disqualified from serious consideration.

The occurrence of private devotions of the priest are of course not unique to East Syria. The missals of the western rite bear witness to the gradual growth and proliferation of private devotions and apologiae for the priest during the Mass, which Bouyer parallels with the East Syrian *kuššāpê*.[2] According to Jungmann, the earliest of such

97

devotions are to be found in the Masses of Mone of the seventh century,[3] and certainly a few are present in the Stowe Missal of the eighth or ninth centuries.[4] In the Egyptian and West Syrian eucharistic rites we see the development of the *accessus ad altare* rites, which convey the ideas of preparation for the sacrifice, and the confession of unworthiness by the priest. We also find a similar development in the *Prothesis* prayer. These various prayers share with the *kuššāpê* Otto's concept of the *mysterium tremendum*,[5] and spring from a similar spirituality or psychology, and may be considered as belonging to the same liturgical genre. Our concern here will be those *kuššāpê* which occur within the anaphora, that is, after the opening dialogue and before the final doxology.

THE TEXTS

As yet we have no critical edition of the East Syrian eucharistic liturgy. The study here is based upon the texts in the Urmiah edition of 1890,[6] the translation found in Brightman,[7] and the Latin version found in Renaudot.[8] In addition, Douglas Webb has kindly drawn my attention to the variant texts which are found in the Chaldean Patriarchate Library Manuscripts 33.22/333 and 209, and also kindly provided me with the Syriac texts of these variants.

The *kuššāpê* which occur in Addai and Mari and in Theodore are identical, and follow exactly the same order, from which it might be inferred that one anaphora depends upon the other for its *kuššāpê*. Those which concern us precede each of the three *kuššāpê* of the anaphoras, and we shall term them 1-3, and that provided for the departed, 4.

The third *kuššāpâ* is provided with a short alternative in some manuscripts, which we shall designate 3a. In Chaldean Patriarchate Library Manuscripts 33.22/333 various parts of 3 and 3a, together with 4, have been run together to form a hybrid prayer. In Chaldean Patriarchate 209, however, we find a different *kuššāpâ* which is addressed to Christ, and which we shall designate 3b, which is followed by one from Nestorius (N1) and a variation on part of 4.

In Nestorius, although the same *kuššāpê* as in Addai and Mari and Theodore occur—and almost invariably written first—much longer alternatives are provided. There are four *ghānātā* in Nestorius, and we shall designate the *kuššāpê* of this anaphora N1 - N4. Whether or not we have here a witness to the existence of at least two different sets of *kuššāpê* originating in different communities can only be matter for speculation. On the whole, the alternatives in Nestorius tend to be lengthier and far more concerned with the celebrant himself than those common to Addai and Mari and Theodore.

ORIGIN AND DATE

In an article concerned with the Malabar rite, published in 1914, Dom R. H. Connolly urged that all prayers bearing the title *kuššâpâ* in the Urmiah text were not part of the traditional liturgy of Addai and Mari.[9] He observed that there is no mention of these whispered prayers in the eucharistic commentaries of Narsai in the fifth century, Bar Lipneh in the seventh century, or even Pseudo-George of Arbel in the tenth century, and it would seem that this silence was sufficient confirmation for Connolly of their intruding character. However, it was left to Edward Ratcliff to popularize this judgment upon the *kuššāpê* in his famous reconstruction of Addai and Mari in 1929, and this view was subsequently endorsed by such distinguished names as Dix and Botte.[10]

What appeared to be based upon the silence of the early East Syrian commentators, and that intuitive feeling which characterizes so much liturgical study, was fortunately put on a more solid basis by W.F. Macomber's publication of the *Mar Eša'ya* text of Addai and Mari in 1966. Macomber observed that the *kuššāpê* prayers were found in the twelfth-century Diabekir *huḏrâ*, but were absent from Mardin 22 and the *Mar Eša'ya* manuscript which he dates in the tenth or eleventh century. Reviewing the evidence, Macomber concluded:

> From this I think it legitimate to conclude that the *kuššāpê* were not generally introduced into the Chaledean Liturgy before the end of the thirteenth century, even though they were in use somewhat earlier in some places. On the other hand, it is quite conceivable that even at the time of the Mar Esa'ya hudra, priests may have said some form of private prayer analogous to our present *kuššāpê* according to their own devotion and without any set formula. One may speculate that perhaps the celebrant would not begin the *ghāntā* until the deacon had stopped chanting. With the introduction of more elaborate chants, this pause would tend to lengthen, and it is easy to imagine that the celebrant would want to fill it with appropriate devotional prayer. One indication of the time when such prayers were fixed in written formulae is the attribution of the final *kuššāpâ* of the Anaphora of Nestorius and its alternate in Chald. Patr. 209 (priests' ritual of the 16th cent.) to the Patriarch Elias III Abu Halim (1176-1190), a noted composer of liturgical prayers.[11]

Here Macomber suggested that the *kuššāpê* may have developed from the introduction of more elaborate chants, and the pause encouraged the celebrant to fill the gap with appropriate devotional prayers. Another possibility is that these prayers originated with the method of choosing the celebrant in the East Syrian rite. Robert Taft, commenting on the dialogue after the Entrance of the Gifts, where the celebrant asks for prayers from his fellow ministers, points out that the Nestorian tradition had a primitive form of concelebration in which only one priest read the eucharistic prayer. The East Syrian custom was for the archdeacon to select just before the anaphora one of the presbyters by turn, for this service.

Taft observes:

> If there were a large number of presbyters, one's turn would occur rarely, and it is understandable that the chosen presbyter, covered with confusion by the great honor conferred on him, would be most effusive in his reverence, expression of unworthiness, and request for the prayers of his concelebrants as he approached the altar.[12]

Taft's observation is made in the context of the evolved rite of departure from the bema and *accessus ad altare*; but perhaps it was precisely this East Syrian practice which gave rise to the anaphoral *kuššāpê*. Not having had time to prepare himself before the liturgy, the chosen celebrant found it necessary to say private prayers during the immediate pre-anaphora and anaphora. Such an idea is suggested by phrases in N4: "Glory to Thee my Lord, who has raised me up at this time to make supplication for Thy people before Thee . . . for Thou hast this day moved me by Thy grace to fall down before Thee at this time."

At what date the *kuššāpê* first appeared in the East Syrian rite it is impossible to say. Macomber, it should be noted, does not suggest a date of origin, but simply suggests that their final incorporation into the manuscripts as fixed forms did not occur before the thirteenth century. Certainly the prayers which have come down to us show all the signs of being highly evolved devotional prayers, incorporating substantial biblical quotation. Nevertheless, it is perhaps questionable as to how much weight should be placed on the omission of the *kuššāpê* from the *Mar Eša'ya* text. Douglas Webb, whose knowledge of the East Syrian manuscripts is matched only by William Macomber, knows of no priests' Ritual in which they do not occur, and points out that it is only in some *huḏrâ* manuscripts that they are omitted, and a tendency of the *huḏrâ* is to abbreviate. Webb has also kindly drawn my attention to the fact that later commentators—John bar Zo'bi, Abdisho of Nisibis, and Timothy II—also tend to pass over the *kuššāpê* yet all the evidence suggests that they were in existence when those writers were at work.[13] The silence of Narsai, Bar Lipneh, and Pseudo-George of Arbel—to which we may now add Gabriel Qatraya—is perhaps not quite so decisive as Connolly and others have concluded. The written *kuššāpê* were quite possibly developments from earlier private extemporary prayers, and commentators would be unlikely to comment upon them.

Whatever may be the date of the composition of the prayers which have come down to us in the manuscripts, the spirituality which they represent can be traced to the fourth and fifth centuries. In a celebrated Note, Edmund Bishop discussed the growth of fear and awe attached to the eucharist, finding the earliest reference in the Mystagogical Catecheses attributed to Cyril of Jerusalem, and which he dated 339 A.D.[14] Various factors have been adduced for this growth: the reaction to Arianism; the developed understanding of the Real Presence; the identification of church buildings with pagan temples and also with the Jerusalem temple; the acceptance of the Old Testament understanding of the holy; and the need to discipline and impress the great influx of semi-pagan converts.[15] Significantly, the language of fear and awe, both in respect to the eucharist and the celebrant, is to be found in three theologians important to the East Syrian tradition—St. John Chrysostom, Theodore of Mopsuestia, and, dependent upon both of these, Narsai.

In *De Sacerdotio* (while of course Chrysostom is speaking mainly of the bishop, the presbyterate were included in the Sacerdotium[16]), Chrysostom stresses that since the soul of the priest should be as a light which shines in the whole world (6.4.524), it is a lofty office.

> Though the office of the priesthood is exercised on earth, it ranks, nevertheless, in the order of celestial things—and rightly so. It was neither man nor an angel nor an archangel nor any created power, but the Paraclete himself who established this ministry, and who ordained that men abiding in the flesh should imitate the ministry of the angels. For that reason it behooves the bearer of the priesthood to be as pure as if he stood in the very heavens amidst those powers. (3.4.175)[17]

The qualities needed by the priest are considerable: dignified, but not haughty; awe-inspiring, but kind; affable in his authority; impartial, but courteous; humble, but not servile; strong, but gentle (3.16.291-292).

Furthermore, the sins of priests will be more severely punished than those of the laity (6.11.574-575). With specific reference to the eucharist, Chrysostom could write:

> When the priest has invoked the Holy Spirit and performed that most awful sacrifice, and constantly handled the Lord of all, where, pray tell me, where shall we rank him? What the purity and what the piety that we shall exact of him? Only think, what manner of hands should they be which perform such a ministry ... There ought to be nothing purer, nothing holier, than the soul which receives so great a spirit. (6.4.519)

Theodore of Mopsuestia, whose writings were more influential for the Nestorians than those of Chrysostom, gives a similar view in his Catechetical Homilies. The minister of baptism and the eucharist is one who has been found worthy of the honor of priesthood.[18] The eucharist is awe-inspiring because the sacred and awe-inspiring body is lying there.[19] The priest is to be in awe and fear more than all, as he is performing for all this service which is so awe-inspiring.[20] He is required to be healthy in his office, and seen to be worthy of the honor he possesses. The *lavabo* is a reminder that all must draw near with a clean conscience.[21] Furthermore, Theodore seems to attest to the beginnings of a rite of *accessus ad altare*.

> After this he offers also thanksgivings for himself for having been appointed servant of such an awe-inspiring Sacrament. With this he prays also for the grace of the Holy Spirit, so that he may be now made by him worthy of the greatness of this service, as he had been rendered by him worthy of priesthood; and so that he may perform this service free, by the grace of God, from all evil conscience, and not fearing any punishment, as he, being infinitely below the dignity of such a service, is drawing nigh unto things that are much higher than himself.[22]

It is hardly surprising that Narsai, who was well acquainted with the writings of Chrysostom and Theodore, should reproduce a very similar spirituality in the liturgical homilies. In Homily 17 he writes:

> The priest now offers the mystery of the redemption of our life, full of awe and covered with fear and great dread. The priest is in awe and great fear and much trembling for his own debts and the debts of all the children of the Church.[23]

Like Chrysostom, Narsai can emphasize the lofty office of the priesthood:

> Let us marvel every moment at the exceeding greatness of thine order, which has bowed down the height and the depth under its authority. The priests of the Church have grasped authority in the height and the depth; and they give commands to heavenly and earthly beings. They stand as mediators between God and man, and with their words they drive out iniquity from mankind.[24]

Indeed, the priest is a mediator between God and the people, and offers spiritual sacrifices to the Lord of all.[25] And Narsai gives a sharp warning against unworthiness of the priest; it behooves the priests more than all others to observe purity, because priests possess an order which is more excellent than all others.[26] Of the unworthy priest, Narsai says:

> And because he has not honoured the excellence of his order as it beseems him, he will there be despised and set at naught before all creatures. Hear, O thou priest, thou hast not works agreeable to thine order; stand in awe and be affrighted at the torment of Gehenna. More grievous than all punishment will be thy punishment, O wicked priest, because thou hast not fittingly administered the order allotted to thee.[27]

Interestingly, in Homily 17 Narsai seems to hint at the East Syrian practice of selecting the celebrant just before the anaphora:

> The priest who is selected to be celebrating this sacrifice, bearing in himself the image of the Lord in that hour . . . Hear, O priest, whither you have been advanced by reason of your order. Stand in awe as it is fitting . . . be without blemish and without blame as it is commanded you.[28]

Here, then, at Antioch, Edessa, and Nisibis in the fourth and fifth centuries, we find the raw material which could give rise to private extemporary prayers, and fore-runners of the written *kuššāpê* which have come down to us in the manuscripts.

THE *Kuššāpê* OF ADDAI AND MARI AND THEODORE

1.   Picking up a theme which occurs in the final *ghāntā* of Addai and Mari, this short *kuššāpâ* is a petition for openness of face in order to accomplish the living and holy service with a clean conscience, using phraseology from Romans 12:1, 2 Corinthians 3:18, Ephesians 3:12, Hebrews 8:18, and 1 Timothy 3:9. The phrase "living and holy service (tešmešā)" does not itself occur in Addai and Mari, but it does

occur in both Theodore and Nestorius, and in the latter it seems to have been derived from a version of the anaphora of St. John Chrysostom.[29]

2.   This *kuššāpâ* represents an embolism or paraphrase of the *Sanctus*. It repeats the special form of the East Syrian *Sanctus*, but expands it to a trinitarian interpretation, comparable with the post-*Sanctus* of Apostolic Constitutions and Basil. It expounds the theme of the theophany of Isaiah 6, with its sense of unworthiness, combined with dread and awe as expressed in Genesis 28:17. It includes a request for purging from uncleanness. The raw material is already found in the comments of Theodore of Mopsuestia and Narsai on the *Sanctus*.[30]

3.   The third *kuššāpâ* as found in Brightman is reminiscent of some sections of the intercessions found in certain West Syrian anaphoras, and in the *Hanc igitur* and *Supplices te* of the Roman Canon, as well as the *kuššāpâ* for the righteous fathers in Addai and Mari. The request that the offering, *qurbānā*, should be accepted, *qbl*, is found in the anaphoras of Theodore and Nestorius, but not Addai and Mari. The offering is offered for a number of groups of people, and again the unworthiness of the priest is stressed.

3a.   The shorter alternative found in some manuscripts, and printed in Renaudot, speaks of the sacrifice offered to "your father"; the term sacrifice, *debhâ*, occurs only in Theodore and Nestorius; Addai and Mari uses only *qurbānā*. The sacrifice is an occasion for a whole number of petitions and requests.

3b.   This implores Christ to have mercy on the church, to accompany the priest, support the orphans and have mercy on the widows, and asks Christ to accept the offering from the hands of the priest.

4.   The *kuššāpâ* of the departed may be used in addition to or in place of the third *kuššāpâ*. While the text in Brightman suggests that this is one long *kuššāpâ*, the use of latter parts in the variants in Chaldean Patriarchate Library 32.22/333 and 209 suggest that we have here two separate *kuššāpê* which have been run together as one. It begins with a declaration of unworthiness, includes petitions, and refers to the sacrifice of Abel, Noah, Abraham, Elijah on Horeb (!), and the widow casting money into the treasury. This particular part is reminiscent of parts of the Anaphora of St. Mark, and one of the preparation prayers in the West Syrian, Maronite, and Armenian rites. The offering is made for the church, priests, rulers, and a variety of categories found in the intercessions of Theodore and Nestorius.

Looking at these together, the first three are prayed by the priest for the church, and in fact they resemble an alternative anaphora, with a sequence: 1 resembles the opening of Nestorius with a petition for the acceptance of the service; 2 resembles the post-*Sanctus* of some West Syrian anaphoras; and 3, the offering with intercession, resembles an anamnesis with intercession. Together they give almost a private anaphora recited at the same time as the public anaphora of the church.

THE *Kuššāpê* OF NESTORIUS

N1. This is similar to the first part of the *kuššāpâ* for the departed. It is a personal prayer of the priest in the first person singular. The mysteries are offered for tranquility in the world, peace, and absolution.

N2. While being an alternative to the post-*Sanctus kuššāpâ* designated 2, this prayer does not pick up on the *Sanctus*, but again is a self-contained prayer in the first person singular. The living and holy sacrifice (*debhtā*) is offered for the priest, and the people for absolution, healing, help, and mercies. It goes on to describe the spiritual fruits of Christ's body and blood mingling with their souls. God is again asked to accept the pure service (*tešmešā*).

N3. Again in the first person singular, this prayer stresses the unworthiness of the minister, and begs for mercy. God is asked to accept the sacrifice, and adoration is offered.

N4. Since Nestorius is divided into four *ghānātā*, a fourth set of *kuššāpê* are provided. The first is in fact the first *ghānātā* of Addai and Mari. The second is a lengthy prayer with a doxological opening, developing into lengthy intercessions for all sorts and conditions of people, ending with a reference to the cherubim and seraphim, and angels of light who sing "holy."

Thus, compared with the *kuššāpê* of Addai and Mari and Theodore, those which are peculiar to Nestorius are more personal—the first person singular—, and they do not form a sequence, but in fact could be placed anywhere without altering their sense.

PRIESTHOOD AND OFFERING

Central to the *kuššāpê* are ideas of priesthood and offering. The priest has been appointed minister and mediator, set apart by God's compassion and mercy (4). Indeed, the very existence of the *kuššāpê* alongside the anaphora emphasizes the mediatory role of the priest. He has been counted among the number and choir of priests; he has been raised up (N4). He is to plead with God for himself and his companions (N3); to intercede and cling to the skirts of God's mercy (N4). "Hear the voice of my complaint" (3a) effectively sums up the suppliant nature of the priesthood.

The theme of the unworthiness of both priest and people runs throughout the *kuššāpê*. The priest pleads for openness of face for the congregation and himself (1), and confesses that he has no openness of face before God (N3). It is interesting that openness of face is, according to the Anaphora of Addai and Mari, precisely one of the gifts of the baptized—"openness of face and unclosed mouth." Possibly the prayers here may be seen an anticipatory; on the other hand, they could be seen as being in direct conflict with the earlier eschatology of Addai and Mari. Another plea of the *kuššāpê* is for being counted worthy (3), whereas the Apostolic Tradition and Justin Martyr give thanks for being counted worthy to stand before God and minister.

In the *kuššāpê* in Nestorius, the emphasis is on the priest pleading for himself. He confesses his frailty (N2). The strongest expression of this is in the third *kuššāpâ* of Nestorius:

> . . . I dust and ashes, a debtor to Thee from the womb, a stranger to Thee from the belly, a dependent on Thee from the bowels of my mother. Pity me in Thy mercies and in Thy compassion draw me out of the sea of debts and in Thy kindness take me out and lift me from the abyss of my sins . . .

Of interest is the apparent Nestorian habit of a triple formula for this unworthiness. In all three East Syrian anaphoras we find the phrase "lowly, weak and miserable sinners," which I have suggested elsewhere is a Nestorian peculiarity.[31] The words do not find a parallel in Maronite *Sharar*, and where similar language does occur, it is in a passage which has no parallel with Addai and Mari, and it uses four adjectives. In the *kuššāpê* we find:

> frailty, misery and poverty (3)
> sinfulness, frailty and poverty (Chald. Pat. 33.22/333)
> sinful and offending and miserable servant (N2)
> sinful, frail and offending servant (N3)

This, I would suggest, gives further support to my contention that the triple formula in Addai and Mari represents an East Syrian devotional formula, and is an addition to the text.

If the priest is an unworthy sinner, nevertheless he is the recipient of the divine grace and mercy. He has been raised up to entreat, supplicate, and plead. He has also been appointed to offer the divine mysteries (4;N1). His task is to accomplish this living and holy service; God is asked to accept the sacrifice (N3) and offering (3) and pure service (N2). The Anaphora of Addai and Mari has a very undeveloped concept of eucharistic offering, and confines itself to the verb *qrb* and the noun *qurbānā*; for praise the verb *slq* is used.[32] The *kuššāpê*, as we might expect, draw freely upon the more developed terminology and concepts found in Theodore and Nestorius—*qbl*, accept, *debhtā*, sacrifice, and *tešmešā*, service.

In conjunction with this offering, the priest entreats, supplicates, and pleads for himself and for all sorts and conditions of people. The third *ghāntā* of Addai and Mari is echoed by 3, and Botte believed that this *kuššāpâ* was originally part of the anaphora.[33] N1 prays for the peace of creation, the upholding of the faithful church, and for the heroic deeds of the priests. The fullest expression is in N4—for those who err, sinners, creation, the afflicted, the harassed, and the departed. It then passes to petitions for the congregation—a whole series of synonymous phrases concerning forgiveness. Last, the priest intercedes for himself, using eschatological language.

> . . . make me a partaker of Thy mysteries and set me with those on the right hand in the world of Thy bliss; make me to sit down in the banqueting hall with those of Thy household; make me to stand boldly before the throne of Thy glory with all Thy saints . . .

REFLECTIONS ON THE ANAPHORAL *Kuššāpê*

I conclude by offering the following brief reflections upon the *kuššāpê*—reflections which are of course limited by the perspectives of a twentieth-century liturgist of the Western Protestant tradition.

1.   The interruption of the anaphora with private asides to God by the priest seems to the modern liturgists entirely out of place. However unworthy the celebrant and the people are, they are nevertheless invited from the highways and byways to share God's banquet. In the anaphora the president articulates the prayer of the people in a sacrifice of praise to the Father. The prayer is prayed by the celebrant on behalf of the church: *we* give thanks, *we* remember, *we* offer, *we* beseech. To interrupt the prayer by private hesitations and personal offering—with an emphasis on "I"—seems to overturn the whole theological function of the eucharistic prayer, and it invites

a distorted view of Christian ministry. This is the very last place in the liturgy which invites individual prayer by the celebrant.

2.   With regard to the concept of eucharistic sacrifice, the *kuššāpê* may be seen as a third stage of development in East Syria. From the undeveloped terminology of Addai and Mari, where the God-ward and human-ward elements are inseparably intertwined, we find a development in the concepts and the articulation of sacrifice in the later anaphoras of Nestorius and Theodore.[34] In the *kuššāpê* the terminology is removed from its proper context—that is, the sacrificial terminology within the framework of a sacrifice of praise in the anaphora—and is thrown together to present an unqualified idea of eucharistic sacrifice, prayed by the priest apart from the *ecclesia*. Like the "Little Canon" of the pre-Vatican II Mass, these prayers tend to pre-empt and undermine the eucharistic offering as it is unfolded in the anaphora. In this sense they are theologically and liturgically undesirable.

3.   Modern liturgical revision has been at pains to emphasize the meal and *koinonia* aspects of the eucharist, and rightly so. But nevertheless, the eucharist is more than a fellowship meal. Here the mighty works of God in word and sacrament are rehearsed, and the grace of God is once more set forth and proclaimed. In a paper entitled "The Function of Contemporary Liturgy," Adrian Jacobs observed that in much modern liturgical revision there is an "over-emphasis on simply instructional comment in liturgical contexts, at the expense of the creation of the sense of the mystery of God, the numinous, the other worldly, in an experience of worship."[35] No one can read the *kuššāpê* of the East Syrian rite without being impressed by their sense of holiness, and the serious nature of the ordained ministry. The minister is more than a cafeteria attendant; his ministry is a sacred ministry, and the communion is *holy* communion. With complete justification the second *kuššāpâ* of Addai and Mari quotes from Genesis: "This is none other than the House of God and this is the Gate of Heaven." And perhaps, therefore, a response of the type made by Job is not out of place:

> I knew of thee then only by report,
> but now I see thee with my own eyes.
> Therefore I despise myself,
> I repent in dust and ashes. (42:5-6)

Karl Barth wrote:

> The actual revelation which we receive in Jesus Christ by the
> Holy Spirit never ceases to tell us that we are sinners, in the

strictest and most serious sense. It is only in and with this judgment upon us, not in ourselves but in Jesus Christ, that we are reconciled with God and therefore sanctified.[36]

In some of our modern eucharistic rites these various elements are missing or muted, and they should not be. Perhaps there is something in these strange East Syrian prayers that we need to listen to and heed. Perhaps there is something in the spirituality of the "Third Stratum" which does, after all, have something to say to the composers of twentieth-century liturgies.

Notes

1. G. Dix, *The Shape of the Liturgy* (London: Dacre Press, Adam and Charles Black, 1945) 522ff.

2. L. Bouyer, *Eucharist*, tr. C.U. Quinn (Notre Dame: University of Notre Dame Press, 1968) 377-378.

3. J. Jungmann, *The Place of Christ in Liturgical Prayer* (London: Geoffrey Chapman, 1965) 254.

4. Text, B. MacCathy, *The Transactions of the Royal Irish Academy* 27 (1886) 144-195; Fol. 29b, Fol. 13a.

5. R. Otto, *The Idea of the Holy* (Harmondsworth: Penguin Books, 1959) 27.

6. *The Liturgy of the Holy Apostles Addai and Mari* (1890) (Syriac text).

7. F.E. Brightman, *Liturgies Eastern and Western*, vol. 1 (Oxford, 1896).

8. E. Renaudot, *Liturgiarum Orientalium Collectio*, vol. 2 (London, 1847).

9. R.H. Connolly, "The Work of Menezes on the Malabar Liturgy," *Journal of Theological Studies* 15 (1913-1914) 396-425, 424.

10. E.C. Ratcliff, "The Original Form of the Anaphora of Addai and Mari: A Suggestion," *Journal of Theological Studies* 30 (1928-1929) 23-32; Dix, *Shape of the Liturgy* 178ff; B. Botte, "L'anaphore chaldéene des apôtres," *Orientalia Christiana Periodica* 15 (1949) 259-276.

11. W.F. Macomber, "The Oldest Known Text of the Anaphora of the Apostles Addai and Mari," *Orientalia Christiana Periodica* 32 (1966) 335-371, esp. p. 347.

12. R. Taft, *The Great Entrance*, Orientalia Christiana Analecta, vol. 200 (Rome: Pontificium Institutum Orientalium Studiorum, 1975) 287.

13. See Albert Khoraiche, "'L'explication de tous les mystères divins' de Yohannan Bar Zo'bi selon le ms. Borg. Syr. 90," *Euntes Docete* 19 (1966) 386-426; D. Webb, "The Mimra on the Interpretation of the Mysteries by Rabban Johannan Bar Zo'bi, and Its Symbolism," *Le Muséon* 88 (1975) 297-326; Jacobus-M. Voste, *Ordo Judiciorum Ecclesiasticorum Collectus Dispositus, Ordinatus et Compositus a Mar Abdiso Metropolita Nisibis et Armeniae* (Vatican: S. Congregazione per la Chiesa Orientalie, 1940) 93-103.

14. E. Bishop, Appendix in R.H. Connolly, *The Liturgical Homilies of Narsai* (Cambridge: Cambridge University Press, 1909) 92-97.

15. Jungmann, *The Place of Christ*; J.G. Davies, "The Introduction of the Numinous into the Liturgy: An Historical Note," *Studia Liturgica* 8 (1971-1972) 216-223.

16. Y. Congar, *Lay People in the Church* (London: Bloomsbury Publishing Co. Ltd., 1960); P.-M. Gy, "Notes on the Early Terminology of Christian Priesthood," in *The Sacrament of Holy Orders* (London: Aquin Press, 1962) 98-115.

17. Quotations are from the edition of W.A. Jurgens, *The Priesthood* (New York: Macmillan Company, 1955).

18. Ed. A. Mingana, Woodbrooke Studies, vol. 6 (Cambridge, 1933) 54.

19. Ibid. 87.

20. Ibid. 102.

21. Ibid. 94.

22. Ibid. 89.

23. Ed. Connolly, *The Liturgical Homilies* 7.

24. Ibid. 48.

25. Ibid. 65-66.

26. Ibid. 70.

27. Ibid. 22.

28. See ibid. 4.

29. See Bryan D. Spinks, "Eucharistic Offering in the East Syrian Anaphoras," *Orientalia Christiana Periodica* 50 (1984) 347-371; reprinted as Chapter 5 of this volume.

30. Mingana, Woodbrook Studies, vol. 6, 118-119; Connolly, *The Liturgical Homilies* 13.

31. Bryan D. Spinks, "The Original Form of the Anaphora of the Apostles: A Suggestion in the Light of Maronite Sharar," *Ephemerides Liturgicae* 91 (1977) 146-161; reprinted as Chapter 2 of this volume.

32. See Spinks, "Eucharistic Offering."

33. B. Botte, "L'anaphore chaldéene"; Botte, "Problèmes de l'anaphore syrienne des apôtres Addai et Mari," *L'Orient syrien* 10 (1965) 89-106.

34. See Spinks, "Eucharistic Offering."

35. *Nashotah Review* 16 (1976) 107-117, p. 111.

36. *Church Dogmatics*, vol. I/1, 363.

8

A Note on the Anaphora Outlined in Narsai's Homily XXXII

PROBABLY ONE OF THE MOST FASCINATING CONTRIBUTIONS IN RECENT YEARS TO the discussion on the pattern of the early eucharistic prayer was the late Professor E.C. Ratcliff's "The Sanctus and the Pattern of the Early Anaphora."[1] In this article Ratcliff compared the anaphora in the Apostolic Tradition with the writings of Justin Martyr and Irenaeus, concluding that the Latin Verona text of the former has been the subject of fourth-century revision. With considerable ingenuity Ratcliff sought to substantiate his belief that the epiclesis of the Apostolic Tradition is a later interpolation, and that originally the prayer consisted of a thanksgiving for creation and a lengthy Christological thanksgiving which, after the institution narrative and the formal anamnesis offering the bread and cup, ended in a final thanksgiving for the admission of the worshipers to share in the worship of heaven (a combination of Daniel 7:10 and Isaiah 6:3), culminating in the *Sanctus* and Amen.[2] The great novelty of Ratcliff's article was the hypothesis that the early anaphora had ended with the *Sanctus*. This erudite study ended thus:

> Here this article reaches its limit. If its contention be sound, it raises a number of questions, most of them depending upon the primary question. Why, if the pattern of the ancient anaphora ever conformed with the reconstruction proposed here, was the pattern abandoned? The surviving literature, and not least the historic liturgies, either supply the answers or offer evidence

> which suggests them. A consideration of the questions and
> answers, however, must be reserved for a future article.[3]

It is greatly to be regretted that the promised article was never
written.

However, the argument was taken a little further in "A Note on the
Anaphoras Described in the Liturgical Homilies of Narsai."[4] Here
Ratcliff argued that the anaphora outlined by Narsai in Homily
XXXII witnessed to an earlier pattern of the anaphora which con-
cluded with the *Sanctus*.

It is with the legitimacy of Ratcliff's interpretation of the brief
reference to the anaphora by Narsai in Homily XXXII that we are
concerned here.

In his essay on Narsai, Ratcliff considered first the anaphora which
is outlined in some detail in Homily XVII. Comparing it with some
aspects of Addai and Mari, Nestorius, and Theodore, he concluded
that "it represents the historic East Syrian anaphoral tradition revised
in such a way as to bring it into closer accord with Greek models. It
belongs, therefore, to the final period in the development of the East
Syrian type of Anaphora."[5] Next, Ratcliff examined a much briefer
outline given in Homily XXI, and interpreted it as a description of a
two-part anaphora, the first part ending with the *Sanctus*, and the
second being mainly concerned with the epiclesis.[6] Finally, Ratcliff
turned to consider the anaphora as outlined in Homily XXXII. Here
we give the text from the translation by R.H. Connolly:

> The priest stands as a tongue to interpret; and his voice preaches
> death and life to men. In the bread and wine he shews the Body
> and Blood of the King who died for the sake of all, and lived and
> gave life to all by His cross. In fear the corporeal being stands to
> minister; and he asks for mercy upon himself and upon his race,
> that it may be made worthy of mercy. And he calls to the Spirit
> to come down to him by the power that is from Him, that he may
> give power in the bread and wine to give life. In the visible bread
> and wine life dwells; and they become food for short-lived
> mortals. With the name of the Divinity—three hypostases—he
> seals his words; and he teaches men to cry "Holy" with the
> spiritual beings.
>
> The people answer after his words: "Holy, Holy, Holy Power,
> hidden from all and revealed to all."[7]

In a footnote to the clause "With the name of the Divinity—three
hypostases—he seals his words," Connolly wrote:

The reference to the Invocation apparently ends here, and the writer turns back to mention the *Sanctus*, which he has passed over. In such a general allusion to the liturgy as this Homily contains this lack of order is no matter for surprise.[8]

It is Connolly's explanation of the reference to the *Sanctus* that Ratcliff disputed:

But, it may be asked, is there, indeed, a lack of order? There is no sign of disorder elsewhere in the exposition . . . Why should Narsai have been confused, when handling that part of the Anaphora with which he was particularly concerned? The answer is simple. Narsai was not confused. He mentions the *Sanctus* at the point where it occurred in the Anaphora which he is expounding. Dom Connolly had clearly assumed that the Anaphora of Homily XXXII must have possessed a Preface and *Sanctus* followed by an Eucharistic Prayer, such as we now have in *Addai and Mari* and other rites eastern and western. There is no warrant for the assumption in the Homily. The Anaphora which the Homily describes was a unity, a single Eucharistic Prayer attaining its end and climax in the invocation and the *Sanctus*.[9]

Drawing upon other Syriac writers—the orthodoxy of some of whom is rather questionable—Ratcliff adduced support for a prayer of a consecratory nature terminating with the *Sanctus*. His final conclusion was that in Homily XXXII Narsai describes the early Syrian pattern of the anaphora which ended with the *Sanctus*; the pattern is already changing in that described in Homily XXI; and in Homily XVII we have the final acceptance of the newer Greek form of the anaphora. This interpretation of the anaphora in Homily XXXII conveniently provided Ratcliff with the much needed support for the hypothesis advanced in the earlier study of the Apostolic Tradition.

A careful scrutiny of Ratcliff's essay on Narsai's homilies reveals that his argument rests upon four main points.

1.   Ratcliff assumed that, in each of the three homilies he considered, Narsai covered the essential contents of the anaphora fully and in proper sequence. Thus he asserted:

A comparison of Homily XVII with the extant liturgical evidence shows Narsai to be a reliable witness to East Syrian usage; he expounds, that is to say, a liturgy actually in use, and one well-known to those for whose benefit the Homily was written. A similar statement may be made about Narsai's Baptismal expositions in Homilies XXI and XXII; wherever their liturgical statements and references can be checked, Narsai's reliability is found to be beyond question. The fact is important. It enables us to accept with confidence Narsai's account of two other Anaphoras which not only differ in shape from each other, but are also strikingly different in arrangement from *Addai and Mari, Theodore* and *Nestorius*.[10]

2.   A second assumption was that the actual text in Homily XXXII, beginning, "The priest stands as a tongue" to "hidden from all and revealed to all," is all concerned with the anaphora. Thus in the words "stands to minister" Ratcliff suggested that we have, perhaps, a direct echo of the earlier part of the anaphora, citing in a footnote clauses from the Apostolic Tradition and Addai and Mari.[11]

3.   Ratcliff appears to have interpreted Narsai's words "With the name of the Divinity—three hypostases—he seals his words" as either referring to, or leading into, the *Sanctus*. Thus:

> When he writes, "With the name of the Godhead, three Hypostases, he [i.e. the priest] seals his words; and teaches men to cry: Holy, with the spiritual beings," Narsai is not saying merely that the *Sanctus* rounds off the invocation or the whole Anaphora; he is referring to a certain relation which is understood by his readers to exist between the invocation of divine power upon the elements and the Seraphic hymn which names and proclaims the three Divine Hypostases. In other words, Narsai, or the Anaphora of Homily XXXII, takes the *Sanctus* as in some way contributing to, or effecting the consecration of the Bread and Wine.[12]

And, referring to two accounts of the consecration of baptismal oil in The History of John the Son of Zebedee, the second of which he regarded as corresponding with the pattern of the anaphora described by Narsai:

> The consecration effected by the *Sanctus* is authentic, because the angelic hymn which imparts it is the utterance, over the elements, of the divinely revealed name of the three Divine Hypostases; the Father, the Son, and the Holy Spirit are respectively named in each utterance of "Holy".[13]

4.   The interpretation of the anaphora in Homily XXXII which Ratcliff offered assumed that there was a precedent for such a pattern. The precedents cited in the essay were two accounts of the consecration of baptismal oil from The History of John the Son of Zebedee. Strangely, Ratcliff made no reference to his earlier article on the Apostolic Tradition, but we may presume that he had this proposed

reconstruction in mind; unless one believed that the early anaphora could conclude with the *Sanctus*, an explanation such as that given by Connolly is more logical and predictable.

It would seem to me that these four main points upon which Ratcliff's explanation is based are extremely dubious. Each point is considered in turn.

1.   In Homily XVII Narsai presents us with an explicit exposition of the eucharistic liturgy, and he therefore described and expounded it in some detail. Even so, the detail is not such that it answers every question concerning the full text of Narsai's rite. In Homily XXII and Homily XXI, Narsai is concerned with the rite of baptism which included first communion. Homily XXII and Homily XXI belong together in that order, for XXII is concerned with the anointing, but the actual baptism and first communion are described in XXI.[14] Since Narsai is not describing just the eucharist in XXI, there is no reason to expect an exposition either as full or as detailed as in the homily devoted solely to that purpose. There is every reason to suppose that the anaphora outlined in Homily XXI is a brief résumé, and certainly not a description of the whole content of the anaphora. However, even if, as Ratcliff claimed, Narsai's reliability in Homilies XVII, XXI, and XXII is beyond question, this does not entitle us to form the same conclusion regarding Homily XXXII without first examining it.

The subject of Homily XXXII is "On the Church and on the Priesthood," and much of it is concerned with the function of the priest. Narsai naturally includes the sacraments of baptism and the eucharist, but an exposition of these two same sacraments is not his purpose. This is most clearly to be seen in his consideration of what the priest does at baptism.

> With the waters of the Spirit he casts them, as in a furnace; and he puts off [from them] iniquity, and puts on the garments of righteousness. He calls and entreats the hidden Power to come down unto him and bestow visible power to give life. The waters become fruitful, as a womb; and the power of grace is like the seed that begets life. Body and soul go down together into the bosom of the water and are born again, being sanctified from defilement.[15]

The remainder of this short section on baptism describes the theological role of the priest in the rite.

From this brief reference, it would be quite ludicrous to claim that here we have a complete and ordered description of the baptismal liturgy known to Narsai. There is no mention of anointing, nor of signing with the threefold name; in fact, taking it literally, we are simply given the order of baptism, invocation, baptism. If Ratcliff's assumptions about the reliability of Narsai on the eucharist in this homily are correct, then they apply equally well to baptism. We would have to conclude that a baptismal rite of baptism in water, an invocation, and a second baptism in water in Homily XXXII suddenly underwent drastic revision by the time Homily XXII and Homily XXI were written. The suggestion is, of course, quite absurd, and represents a misuse of the homiletic material; clearly the baptismal liturgy is not being described in any detail at all. But this is true also of the eucharist. There are no grounds for assuming that an anaphora is being described accurately in detail. Rather, the eucharistic rite is alluded to simply to describe in general terms the function and power of the priest.

2.   From the beginning of his essay on Narsai, Ratcliff assumed that in Homily XXXII, where the eucharistic rite is being alluded to, it is the anaphora which is being outlined. This might suggest itself from the mention of the epiclesis and the *Sanctus*, but as we have seen, Ratcliff suggested that the words "stands to minister" were perhaps an echo of the first part of the anaphora. However, it seems equally possible, especially if reference is made to Homily XVII, that the first part of the text is not at all concerned with the anaphora, but with the action and function of the priest before the anaphora. Thus:

> (a) The priest stands as a tongue to interpret; and his voice preaches death and life to men. In the bread and wine he shews the Body and Blood of the King who died for the sake of all, and lived and gave life to all by His cross.

Homily XVII

> The priest now offers the mystery of the redemption of our life, full of awe and covered with fear and great dread . . . He is the eye of the whole ecclesiastical body; and he makes remembrance in his mind of the doings of all his fellow-servants. He is also the tongue of the whole body of Jesus; he is an attorney (συνηγορία), and fills an advocacy (ἐπίτροπος) on its behalf . . . The awful King, mystically slain and buried, and the awful watchers, standing in fear in honour of their Lord.[16]

Homily XXI

> With the pen of his word he draws an image of the crucified King; and as with the finger he points out His passion, also His

exaltation. Death and life his voice proclaims in the ears of the people; and forgiveness of iniquity he distributes, he gives, in the Bread and the Wine. A mystery of death he shews first to mortal man; and then he reveals the power of life that is hidden in his words.[17]

(b) In fear the corporeal being stands to minister;

Homily XVII (having emphasized the fear and awe)

In this frame of mind stands the priest to officiate, reverent, with great fear and trembling.[18]

(c) and he asks for mercy upon himself and upon his race, that it may be made worthy of mercy.

Homily XVII

He asks prayer of the deacons that are round about him, that by his humility he may receive mercy from the Merciful. He now prays with a contrite heart before God, and confesses his debts and the debts of the ecclesiastical body.[19]

These possible similarities all occur before the anaphora as outlined in Homily XVII, and in the singular instance quoted of Homily XXI. For reasons which will be explained later, it could well be the case that the only references to the actual anaphora in Homily XXXII are to the epiclesis and the *Sanctus*. We suggest that the material before the mention of the epiclesis deals with the priest's function in the pre-anaphora.

3.   According to Ratcliff, the clause "With the name of the Divinity—three hypostases—he seals his words" is a lead in for the *Sanctus*, and he cited other Syriac works to support this understanding of "the name of the Divine—three hypostases." Whatever be the case concerning the other works cited, it would seem from the four liturgical homilies translated by Connolly that Narsai had his own consistent definition of the phrase "name of the Divinity—three hypostases."

In Homily XVII Narsai explains:

The three hypostases the Church learned from our Saviour— Father and Son and Holy Spirit—one Divinity; three hypostases, of which none is prior to or later than another, and there is no distinction, save only as to the properties—fatherhood, and generation, and procession—one will, one glory, one lordship: a mystery which is altogether hidden and concealed and covered over away from all; and the watchers are too feeble to examine the secret thereof.[20]

Narsai certainly regarded the "one Divinity, three hypostases" as having spiritual power; thus in Homily XXII:

> The name of the Divinity he mixes in his hands with the oil; and he signs and says "Father" and "Son" and "Holy Spirit." "Such a one," he says, "is signed with the three names that are equal, and there is no distinction of elder or younger between One and Another."
>
> . . . By the visible oil he shews the power that is in the names, which is able to confirm the feebleness of men with hidden [powers]. The three names he recites together with [the rubbing of] the oil upon the whole man; that hostile demons and vexing passions may not harm him. It is not by the oil that he keeps men from harms: it is the power of Divinity that bestows power upon [its] feebleness.[21]

However, there seems to be no sound reason for interpreting the naming of the Divinity, the three hypostases, as being the recitation of the *Sanctus*. Narsai seems to mean simply the naming of the Trinity—Father, Son, and Holy Spirit. Thus in Homily XXXII:

> "Go forth," said He, "and make disciples and preach and baptise all peoples!" [teaching them] the one Divinity of the one Creator, three hypostases. The three names he is bound to preach in the ears of men, and to cause them to think upon the name of the Divinity that is hidden from all.[22]

It is clear that this refers not to the *Sanctus* but to the naming of the Father, Son, and Holy Spirit in Matthew 28:19. This is illustrated further in Homily XXI. Referring to baptism Narsai says:

> With the name of the Divinity, the three Names (Mosul MS, three hypostases} he consecrates the water, that it may suffice to accomplish the cleansing of the defiled. The defilement of men he cleanses with water: yet not by the water, but by the power of the name of the Divinity which there lights down.[23]

And slightly further on:

> Of the name of the Divinity he makes mention, and he says three times: "Father and Son and Holy Spirit, one equality." The names he repeats with the voice openly, and thus he says: "Such a one is baptized in the name of the Father and the Son and the Spirit."[24]

Of immediate significance for the clause of Homily XXXII under discussion is a reference which occurs in Homily XXI regarding the eucharist:

He breaks the Bread and casts [it] into the Wine, and he signs and says: "In the name of the Father and the Son and the Spirit, an equal nature."

With the name of the Divinity, three hypostases, he completes his words; and as one dead he raises the Mystery, as a symbol of the verity.[25]

One cannot fail to notice the striking similarity between the words italicized and the clause of Homily XXXII. In Homily XXI it comes after the anaphora at the commixture, and, apparently, before the Lord's Prayer. Narsai seems to suggest that the eucharistic action of the priest is not completed (or sealed) until the commixture. He explains the latter:

In verity did the Lord of the Mystery rise from the midst of the tomb; and without doubt the Mystery acquires the power of life. On a sudden the bread and wine acquire new life; and forgiveness of iniquity they give on a sudden to them that receive them. He [the priest] makes the Bread and Wine one by participation, forasmuch as the blood mingles with the body in all the senses [of man]. Wine and water he casts into the cup before he consecrates, forasmuch as water also is mingled with the blood in things created.[26]

This action is completed by the recitation of the words "In the name of the Father and the Son and the Spirit, an equal nature." This is confirmed by Homily XVII:

He breaks the Bread in the name of the Father and Son and Spirit, and unites the Blood with the Body, and the Body with the Blood. He signs the Blood with the Body, and makes mention of the Trinity: and he signs the Body with the living Blood with the same utterance. He unites them—the Body with the Blood, and the Blood with the Body—that everyone may confess that the Body and the Blood are one.[27]

In light of this, there is good reason to suppose that the clause "With the name of the Divinity . . ." refers not to the ending of the anaphora, but to the completion of the priest's action in the rite by the commixture when he makes mention of the Trinity.

4.   It has been observed that in support of his interpretation of the anaphora Ratcliff cited two baptismal accounts from The History of John the Son of Zebedee. In both these accounts the *Sanctus* is mentioned; but we may question the legitimacy of concluding that in *both* instances the *Sanctus* formed part of the rite and effected the consecration.

The first citation was from the account of the baptism of Tyrannus. At the consecration of the oil, after John had invoked the Trinity three times, we are informed:

> And straightway fire blazed forth over the oil, and the oil did not take fire, for two angels had their wings spread over the oil and were crying, "Holy, holy, holy, Lord Almighty."[28]

And after signing the water in the name of the Trinity:

> And the whole people cried, "Amen." And straightway these two angels came and hovered over the water, and were crying, "Holy, holy, holy, Father and Son and Spirit of holiness", after him. And St. John cried after them, "Amen".[29]

It will be noticed that in this narrative the *Sanctus* follows the naming of the Trinity, but in both cases it is sung by two angels, not the congregation. The implication would seem to be that when in the baptismal rite the Trinity was named, there was a heavenly counterpart, namely, the angels singing the *Sanctus*. This would seem to be regarded as ratification in heaven of the earthly consecration effected by the recitation of the name of the Trinity. It is not necessarily implied that the *Sanctus* formed part of the earthly rite.[30]

The second citation was from the account of the baptism of the priests of Artemis. Here the oil and water seem to have been consecrated together:

> And in that hour fire blazed forth over the oil, and the wings of the angels were spread forth over the oil; and the whole assemblage was crying out, men and women and children, "Holy, holy, holy, Lord Almighty, of whose praises heaven and earth are full." And straightway the vision was taken away.[31]

The reference here to "vision" again raises the question of whether the *Sanctus* was actually part of the rite, or whether it was simply believed to be the heavenly counterpart to an invocation of the Trinity. However, even if we accept that in this second instance Ratcliff's understanding of the narrative is correct, and that the congregation did say the *Sanctus*, one must still question the validity of arguing from a single instance of consecrating baptismal oil to the shape of the anaphora.[32] What is required is an authentic anaphora which terminates with the *Sanctus*; this is supplied neither by the narrative of the baptism of the priests of Artemis, nor by Ratcliff's reconstruction of the Apostolic Tradition.

Having outlined objections to Ratcliff's interpretation of the anaphora in Homily XXXII, we are now in a position to outline our own interpretation.

From what has been said above, it will be apparent already that we do not accept that the passage in question does refer solely to the anaphora. Bearing in mind the vague references to baptism in the same homily, we suggest that much of the text is concerned with the function of the priest in the eucharistic rite as a whole, and these general statements echo some passages of Homilies XVII and XXI which describe the pre-anaphora. In the light of a very similar clause in Homily XXI, we suggest that the clause concerning the naming of the Divinity refers to the *In nomine Patris* at the commixture, which for Narsai was necessary for the completion of the rite before communion. The reference to the calling down of the Spirit is obviously concerned with the epiclesis of the anaphora—indeed, judging from the other homilies, Ratcliff was correct to point out Narsai's obsession with the epiclesis.

What then of the reference to "he teaches men to cry 'Holy' with the spiritual beings"? It would seem that there are two possible explanations.

In the light of the suggested interpretation of the "name of the Divinity," the first possible explanation suggests itself from Homily XXI. After the commixture and the Lord's Prayer, Narsai describes the people's response:

> With the voice of praise they seal the words of the completion of the Mysteries; and they render holiness to the Father and to the Son and to the Holy Spirit; "Holy is the Father, and holy is His Begotten, and the Spirit who is from Him [*sc.* the Father]; and to them is due holiness and praise from all mouths.[33]

This may be compared with the corresponding section in Homily XVII:

> And when the children of the Church have been prepared to receive the Mysteries, the priest cries out: "To the holy ones is the Holy Thing fitting". To all the holy ones, sanctified by the Spirit of adoption of sons, is the Holy Thing fitting by the consensus of the Fathers . . .

> The people answer: "One is the Father, that Holy One who is from eternity, without beginning and without end; and as a favour He hath made us worthy to acquire sanctification from the spiritual birth of baptism. And one is the Father, and one also

> is the Son and the Holy Spirit: one in three and three in one, without alteration. Glory to the Father, and to the Son who is from Him, and to the Holy Spirit, a Being who is for ever and ever without end."[34]

An abbreviation of the *Hagia Hagiois* may underlie Narsai's reference in Homily XXXII.

The second possible explanation is that it is in fact a reference to the *Sanctus* recited by the people within the anaphora, and, as Dom Connolly suggested, Narsai turns back to mention it. The formula given approximates more to the *Sanctus* than to the response to the *Hagia Hagiois*. Furthermore, there is a verbal similarity with Narsai's explanation of the *Sanctus* in Homily XXI:

> He imitates the spiritual beings by his words while he is making supplication; and holily he *teaches* the people *to cry "Holy"*. The utterance of sanctification of the heavenly beings he recites to men, that they may be crying: "Holy, Holy, Holy, Lord".[35]

There is good reason for the epiclesis and the *Sanctus* to be the only parts of the anaphora mentioned; the reason is hinted at by Edmund Bishop in the Appendix to Connolly's translation. Bishop carefully noted that after the *Sursum corda* the canon seems to have been recited silently except for three things: the concluding words of the preface which led into the *Sanctus*; at the signing of the mysteries when the people said "Amen"; and after the epiclesis, when "the priest makes his voice to be heard to all the people, and signs with his hand over the mysteries, as before," but now "to teach . . . that they are accomplished."[36] Since Narsai was concerned to describe the priest's theological function in the eucharist, he would naturally mention the epiclesis—even though it appears to have been recited silently— since he regarded this as the moment of consecration. This was at the center of the priest's function. But Narsai might be expected to turn back to give some explanation of what for the congregation must have been the most significant and puzzling interruptions of the silent canon, namely, the recitation of the *Sanctus*. What explanation could be given for this curious interruption, for the *Sanctus* plays no obvious theological role in the consecration? What obvious significance could Narsai give for the *Sanctus*? Simply that the priest raises his voice to give the congregation the cue for reciting it; that is, "he teaches men to cry 'Holy' with the spiritual beings. The people answer after his words: Holy, Holy, Holy Power, hidden for all and revealed to all."

The explanation of the *so-called* anaphora in Homily XXXII offered here is, admittedly, not as fascinating as that suggested by Ratcliff, but it gives some consistency to the eucharistic material in the liturgical homilies of Narsai; it also avoids the unlikely conclusion of drastic liturgical revolutions at Edessa and Nisibis during the latter part of the fifth century.

Notes

1. E.C. Ratcliff, "The Sanctus and the Pattern of the Early Anaphora," *Journal of Ecclesiastical History* 1 (1950) 29-36, 125-134.

2. Ibid. 133-134.

3. Ibid. 134.

4. E.C. Ratcliff, "A Note on the Anaphoras Described in the Liturgical Homilies of Narsai," in *Biblical and Patristic Studies in Memory of Robert Pierce Casey*, ed. J.N. Birdsall and R.W. Thompson (Freiburg: Herder, 1963) 235-249.

5. Ibid. 237.

6. Ibid. 238-240.

7. *The Liturgical Homilies of Narsai*, translated into English with an Introduction by R.H. Connolly. With an Appendix by Edmund Bishop, Texts and Studies, vol. 8, no. 1 (Cambridge: Cambridge University Press, 1909) 67.

8. Ibid. 67, note 1.

9. Ratcliff, "A Note" 244.

10. Ibid. 237.

11. Ibid. 244.

12. Ibid. 245.

13. Ibid. 247.

14. Connolly, *The Liturgical Homilies* xlvii.

15. Ibid. 66.

16. Ibid. 7.

17. Ibid. 55.

18. Ibid. 7.

19. Ibid. 7-8.

20. Ibid. 13.

21. Ibid. 44-45; cf. p. 42.

22. Ibid. 65.

23. Ibid. 50.

24. Ibid. 51; cf. p. 41.

25. Ibid. 59.

26. Ibid.

27. Ibid. 23.

28. W. Wright, *Apocryphal Acts of the Apostles*, 2 vols. (London, 1871); reproduced in E.C. Whitaker, *Documents of the Baptismal Liturgy*, 2d ed. (London: SPCK, 1970) 21-22.

29. Ibid.

30. Narsai seems to suggest that the *Sanctus* is the divine proof text of the unity of the Trinity which is confessed on earth (Connolly, *The Liturgical Homilies* 13).

31. Whitaker, *Documents* 21.

32. The Acts of Judas Thomas, which according to A.F.J. Klijn were probably written at Edessa in the beginning of the third century (and from which Ratcliff quoted in another context in his essay), give no support for the consecration or invocation concluding with the *Sanctus*, although the Greek version of the baptism of Gundaphorus does have a consecration ending with the naming of the Trinity. Logically, if Ratcliff's interpretation is correct, we should expect to find the *Sanctus* in Narsai's accounts of baptism. On the whole, where the *Sanctus* does occur in baptismal *ordines*, it seems to be a later interpolation from the eucharistic anaphora (S.P. Brock, "Studies in the Early History of the Syrian Orthodox Baptismal Liturgy," *Journal of Theological Studies*, New Series, 23 (1972) 16-64, esp. pp. 40-43). The occurrence in the *ordo* of Timothy of Alexandria, which might appear to give support, is not a true parallel since the *Sanctus* is connected with the exorcism of the water, and the prayer(s) of consecration continue after its recitation (S.P. Brock, "A New Syriac Baptismal *Ordo* Attributed to Timothy of Alexandria," *Le Muséon* 83 (1970) 367-431; the text of the relevant prayers with translation, pp. 383-386).

33. Connolly, *The Liturgical Homilies* 60.

34. Ibid. 26-27.

9

The East Syrian Anaphoras and Current Liturgical Revision

UNLIKE THE ANAPHORA OF HIPPOLYTUS, WHICH IF IT WAS EVER USED WIDELY (IT is an episcopal ordination eucharistic prayer, not an ordinary Sunday eucharistic prayer) fell into disuse, and is something of a museum piece which modern revisers have resurrected,[1] the East Syrian anaphoras are still in regular use today. All three are used by the Church of the East and the Chaldean Catholics, and that of Addai and Mari is in use in the Syro-Malabar Church of India. Generally speaking, the Church of the East is content with this liturgical heritage, as are the Chaldeans with their slightly modified texts. Less satisfaction is manifested in parts of the Syro-Malabar Church.

The East Syrian anaphoras have not escaped unscathed from "westernization." In India the Portuguese were responsible for the suppression of the anaphoras of Theodore and Nestorius on the grounds that they were written by heresiarchs. Addai and Mari provided a problem since it lacked what the fifteenth- and sixteenth-century Latin West regarded as crucial, namely, the words of institution. *Vat. Syr. 66* of Mar Joseph Sulaqa contains the first signs of westernization. An institution narrative with a slight Latin flavor was written on a separate folio at the beginning of the liturgy, with a note that they were to be recited probably after the fraction and consignation.[2] In both the Menezian and Rozian liturgies the narrative is included after the anaphora and before the fraction.[3] Here we

125

encounter western concern for form and matter of sacraments, and an uncertainty about the validity of the Anaphora of Addai and Mari.

The same western concern was seen in the Chaldean Catholic missals where in 1901 and 1936 an institution narrative was inserted within the anaphora in the middle of the post-*Sanctus*, and the Archbishop of Canterbury's Mission also included 1 Corinthians 11:23-25 in its 1890 Urmiah edition. One might also cynically remark that those who have argued so strongly for a "missing" institution narrative in Addai and Mari have received theological formation in a communion where such words are regarded as crucial for a valid eucharist. However, none of these attempts have been wholly convincing. The fact remains that there is no manuscript authority for the insertion of an institution narrative, and unless one approaches this ancient anaphora with *a priori* views on "consecration," the thought sequence of the anaphora does not demand one. Enrico Mazza has rightly concluded:

> Whatever theories historian may elaborate, there is no disputing that an entire Church—the Chaldean or East Syrian—has lived for centuries with an anaphora of that archaic type which does not contain an account of institution but simply refers to the institution; we mean the Chaldean Anaphora of the Apostles Addai and Mari. Furthermore, no one wants to or can deny the validity of the Eucharist that has been celebrated for centuries in the Chaldean Church. What arguments could possibly justify denying that the legitimate tradition of this Church is also a completely valid tradition?[4]

Of the attempts to supply a narrative, the Syro-Malabar solution seems to be the less offensive—a narrative is recited near the fraction before the communion "just in case" the anaphora is deficient, whereas the insertion of a narrative within the anaphora is a declaration that the received text is deficient. But any deficiency or doubt is a western judgment based upon western theological presuppositions; it is not an eastern judgment.

In light of this, it is understandable that there has been some controversy in the Syro-Malabar Church regarding the 1989 revision of the *qurbānā*.[5] After centuries of westernization or Latinization, there has been a movement in this Church to return to the "purer" East Syrian tradition, and this has received encouragement from Rome. However, others have felt that after four hundred years of a hybrid rite, the "pure" East Syrian tradition is now alien to the Syro-Malabar Church, and any reform should begin from the hybrid rites, not from a restoration of forms which were suppressed in the sixteenth century. The 1989 *Qurbana* represents something of a compromise and has pleased few. The Anaphora of Addai and Mari has been modified to include a post-*Sanctus* and institution narrative inspired by Theodore and Nestorius:

> And with these heavenly hosts we give you thanks, O Lord, and we bless God the word, hidden offspring from your bosom, who, being in your likeness and the splendour which is from you and the image of your being, thought this not robbery to be your equal, but emptied himself and took the likeness of a servant and became man perfect with a rational and intelligent and immortal soul and with a mortal human body, and was born of a woman and was under the law that he might redeem those who were under the law, and he left unto us the memorial of our salvation, this mystery which we offer before you.

> O Lord my God, we make the memorial of the passion of your Son as he taught us. On the night he was betrayed Jesus took bread in his pure and holy hands, lifted up his eyes to heaven, towards you, his glorious father and blessed it, broke and gave it to his disciples and said: this is my body which is broken for you for the forgiveness of sins. Take and eat of it all of you. Amen.

> And likewise over the cup he gave thanks and blessed and gave it to them and said: this is my blood of the new covenant, which is shed for many for the forgiveness of sins. Take and drink of it, all of you. Amen.

> When you are gathered together in my name, do in remembrance of me this that I have done.[6]

Here the type of institution narrative is that which Botte argued for, based upon that of Theodore, and Philippians 2:5-11 has been used. It is true that this is "authentically East Syrian." The manhood and obedience of Christ were extremely important in the Christology of Theodore of Mopsuestia and Nestorius, and Philippians 2:5-11 is important in their expositions, and it is used in both the anaphoras of Theodore and Nestorius. The institution narrative is also Syrian, since Botte showed its antecedents in Aphrahat and Ephraem.[7] Whether this expansion of Addai and Mari represents a legitimate modern revision is no doubt debatable. Some members of the Syro-Malabar Church would argue that it may be "authentically East Syrian" in flavor, but that what is needed is an "authentic Indian" revision of Addai and Mari, and that this revision is once more a western imposition.

It is probably inconceivable that current Roman Catholic and Anglican eucharistic prayers would not contain an institution narrative, and one can again see behind the Syro-Malabar revision the western concern for the inclusion of the narrative. Given the antiquity of Addai and Mari, perhaps the best policy would be to leave it intact for those Eastern Churches which use it, as a witness to an earlier age when disputes about form and matter and valid consecration had not begun. Its survival many be an uncomfortable fact which the west must live with. On the other hand, the 1989 Syro-Malabar revision could be authorized for use in the west as a legitimate modern western revision of an ancient eastern text, in much the same way as new anaphoras have been based directly upon Hippolytus. This would be quite different from a western revision for eastern usage, which is what the 1989 text is discerned as being.

A rather different and lighter approach is to be found in Eucharistic Prayer C of the Church of England's *Patterns for Worship* 1989. This prayer (which like all four eucharistic prayers in this collection has not yet received Synodical authorization for legal regular use) is as follows:

> Lord God of justice and mercy,
> you care for the world and for every child of your creation;
> we glorify your Name.
> You call us to share your life and you give us your love.
> You are our father, kind and compassionate,
>   always ready to forgive.
> You rejoice in our joy, listen patiently to our troubles,
>   and comfort us in distress.
>
> You show your love in Jesus Christ your Word made flesh.
> He is your Good News to the World; through him we are saved.
> He gave up his life on the cross to be a ransom for many.
>
> At supper the night before he died, he took bread and broke it,
> giving you thanks and praise.
> He gave it to his disciples and said:
> "This is my body given for you".
>
> And the end of supper he took the cup of wine and said:
> "This cup is the New Covenant in my blood.
> Drink it in remembrance of me".
>
> God of all holiness, we are gathered in your Name to celebrate the sacrifice Jesus made for us all, and to praise you for his glorious resurrection. As we do this in remembrance of him, may your Spirit show these gifts of bread and wine to be for us his saving body and blood.

Lord and giver of life, help us to work together for your kingdom, and for that day when your justice and mercy will be seen by all the world.

By your grace unite us in Christ with your whole Church in earth and in heaven so that with one voice we may worship you and praise your Name:

Holy, holy, holy is the Lord God Almighty,
Who was, and is and is to come.
To him be honour and glory for ever and ever. Amen.

This prayer has optional responses, and the traditional *Sanctus* can be used after "comfort us in distress."

A mere textual comparison with Addai and Mari will show little correlation. However, the phraseology has been quite deliberately transposed into English idiom in the new prayer.

1. "We glorify your Name." Confer *Sharar*, "Glory to you, the adorable and glorious Name."

2. "You call us to share your life and you give us your love." This is a modern English paraphrase of "you put on our humanity so as to quicken us by your divinity."

3. "Kind and compassionate." Confer "created . . . its inhabitants in his compassion, and redeemed mankind in his mercy."

4. "We are gathered in your Name to celebrate the sacrifice Jesus made for us all." Confer "And we also, O Lord . . . who are gathered together . . . the example which is from you."

5. "May your Spirit show these gifts of bread and wine to be for us his saving body and blood." "Show" is from St. Basil, but "gifts," also from St. Basil, is a counterpart of *qurbānā*, offering, and "saving body and blood" represents a précis of the eschatological fruits of communion.

6. "By your grace unite us in Christ and with your whole Church." Confer "we give you thanks and praise you without ceasing in your Church."

The eucharistic prayer ends with the opening theme of praise of the Name.

Here is an attempt to render some of the thought forms of Addai and Mari/*Sharar* into a modern English prayer. It is not a modernized version of Addai and Mari, but takes its inspiration from this ancient prayer.

What of Theodore and Nestorius? Vadakkel has provided a critical text of Theodore,[8] and I am given to understand that a critical text of Nestorius has now been completed as a doctoral study in Rome, and is likely to be published. What have hitherto been provisional judgments upon these anaphoras can now give way to more confident estimations.

Both Anglicans (1890) and Chaldeans (1901) suppressed the names of Theodore and Nestorius in their editions, simply calling them the second and third hallowings. This might have been justified if these anaphoras were deliberately polemical and heterodox. In fact, this is not so. Since Nestorius is based upon Syro-Byzantine anaphoras and Addai and Mari, it would seem difficult to object to it, though the name Nestorius which is attached to it is problematical for Chalcedonian Churches. There should be less of a problem over Theodore. It may be true that the seeds for Nestorianism are sown in Theodore, but in his day he was regarded as Orthodox, and as a champion of Antiochene Christology with its concern for the true humanity of Christ. To visit the sins of the sons upon the father seems a little unjust, particularly when the father was held in high esteem in his own generation. Those phrases in these two anaphoras which scholars such as William Bright thought might reflect Nestorianism are in fact the ancient Syriac expression for the incarnation.[9]

Use of ancient anaphoras simply by way of modern translation is rarely successful. It is doubtful whether any modern Western Church would want to use or benefit from use of either of these two anaphoras. However, the *shape* of these East Syrian anaphoras deserves to be considered, together with their concern for the incarnation and true humanity of our Lord. The Syro-Byzantine and Egyptian shapes of the anaphora have been utilized in modern revisions, but so far as I am aware, not the East Syrian with its distinct sequence in Theodore and Nestorius of institution narrative, intercessions, and then epiclesis. I have argued elsewhere that this gives classic expression to the eucharistic theology of Theodore of Mopsuestia.[10] However, the two are not inseparable.

The Syro-Byzantine shape of the anaphora uses the institution narrative as the final part of the Christological thanksgiving, and gives way to supplication, first by way of the epiclesis for consecration and the fruits of communion, and then for the church, living and departed. The East Syrian anaphora also concludes its thanksgiving with the institution narrative, but in the Christological thanksgiving makes use of Philippians 2:5-11. The narrative of institution anchors the obedient manhood of Philippians in the sacrifice on the cross, and thereafter the vicarious manhood of Christ is pleaded in the intercessions, love and concern for the neighbor (as befits a servant Christology) coming before a personal concern for consecration and the fruits of communion. The vicarious humanity of Christ has been significant in a number of modern Christologies, and has been championed in particular by T.F. Torrance and J.B. Torrance.[11] The work of the vicarious humanity of Christ is based upon the twin moments in salvation of substitution/representation and incorporation. Christ not only takes our place and becomes our representative, thereby creating a new humanity, but also incorporates us into this new humanity. Our actions become his actions. Our life becomes his life, the life of God. Even if this is not all that can be said about Christology, it is an important aspect, and it can be given liturgical expression by using the shape of the East Syrian anaphoras, and their use of Philippians 2:5-11. These East Syrian anaphoras may yet prove useful for modern western anaphoral revision.

Notes

1. For example, Eucharistic Prayer 2 of the Missal of Paul VI; Eucharistic Prayer 3 of the Church of England Alternative Service Book 1980.

2. A. Raes, "Le récit de l'institution eucharistique dans l'anaphore chaldéenne et malabare des apôtres," *Orientalia Christiana Periodica* 10 (1944) 216-226; Placid of S. Joseph, "The Present Syro-Malabar Liturgy: Menezian or Rozian?" *Orientalia Christiana Periodica* 23 (1957) 313-331.

3. Raes, "Le récit."

4. Enrico Mazza, *The Eucharistic Prayers of the Roman Rite* (New York: Pueblo, 1986) 258.

5. Jacob Vellian, *Syro-Malabar Liturgy*, vol. 1, *Raza: The Most Solemn Qurbānā* (Kottayam: St. Joseph's Press, 1989); Bryan D. Spinks, "Syrian versus Hindu Conflict over Inculturation in India," in *Liturgical Inculturation in the Anglican Communion*, ed. David R. Holeton, Alcuin/Grow Liturgical Study, vol. 15 (Bramcote: Grove Books, 1990) 46-48; F. Kanichikattil, *To Restore or to Reform* (Bangalore: Dharmaram Publications, 1922.

6. Text, Vellien, *Raza*, Appendix 39-40.

7. B. Botte, "L'anaphore chaldéenne des apôtres," *Orientalia Christiana Periodica* 15 (1949) 259-276.

8. Jacob Vadakkel, *The East Syrian Anaphora of Mar Theodore of Mopsuestia* (Kottayam: Oriental Institute of Religious Studies, India, 1989).

9. B.J. Kidd, ed., *Letters of William Bright, D.D.* (London: Wells, Gardner, Darton & Co., 1903); more details are given in Chapter 7 of my forthcoming Placid Lectures, *Western Use and Abuse of the Eastern Liturgical Traditionalism: Some Cross-Sections in Its History* (Rome: Centre for Indian and Inter-Religious Studies, 1993).

10. Bryan D. Spinks, "The East Syrian Anaphora of Theodore: Reflections upon Its Sources and Theology," *Ephemerides Liturgicae* 103 (1989) 441–455; reprinted as Chapter 4 of this volume.

11. Christian D. Kettler, *The Vicarious Humanity of Christ and the Reality of Salvation* (Maryland and London: University Press of America, 1991); T.F. Torrance, *The Mediation of Christ* (Edinburgh: T. & T. Clark, 1992); see also *Christ in Our Place: The Humanity of God in Christ for the Reconciliation of the World*, ed. T. Hart and D. Thimell (Exeter: The Paternoster Press, 1991).